Cocktail Guide
for Connoisseurs

In this series:

© h.f.ullmann publishing GmbH
Original title: *Cocktail Guide für Kenner*
ISBN of the original edition: 978-3-8480-0691-5

Editing and proofreading, layout, and typesetting: Christian Heße & Martina Schlagenhaufer
Graphic design: Erill Fritz, Berlin
Project management: Isabel Weiler
Cover photo: © h.f.ullmann publishing GmbH/Faber & Partner, Thomas Pothmann

© for the English edition: h.f.ullmann publishing GmbH

Translation from German: Ann Drummond, Rosemary Lawrey and Katherine Taylor in
association with First Edition Translations Ltd, Cambridge
Editing: Jenny Knight in association with First Edition Translations Ltd, Cambridge
Typesetting: The WriteIdea in association with First Edition Translations Ltd, Cambridge

Overall responsibility for production: h.f.ullmann publishing GmbH, Potsdam, Germany

Printed in Italy, 2014

ISBN 978-3-8480-0692-2

10 9 8 7 6 5 4 3 2 1
X IX VIII VII VI V IV III II I

www.ullmann-publishing.com
newsletter@ullmann-publishing.com
facebook.com/ullmann.social

André Dominé (Editor)

Cocktail Guide
for Connoisseurs

TEXT

André Dominé & Matthias Stelzig

PHOTOGRAPHY

Armin Faber & Thomas Pothmann

h.f.ullmann

8 Preface

10 From al-kuhl to cocktail
André Dominé

32 Location bar
Matthias Stelzig

54 Behind the bar

Matthias Stelzig

84 Cocktails and drinks

André Dominé & Matthias Stelzig

214 Endmatter

Preface

Cocktail—a word to conjure up associations, images, and memories. Something refreshing and stimulating always springs to mind, rather than any sense of loneliness or quiet isolation. Instead, we imagine a lively scene where it's all happening, with pulsating music to swing along to, where we can share experiences with others. Cocktails suggest mood, ambiance, and conviviality, and they always involve a high level of creativity as well.

Various things combine to make a cocktail. It needs at least two ingredients, one of which supplies the stronger kick. More is not always better, though it can be, especially when visual appeal is also part of the equation. Cocktails are creations. Taste is the main thing, of course, but it won't work if it doesn't look good. It can be so simple, and simply perfect, like a Mojito or Caipirinha: green peppermint leaves swirling among sparkling ice cubes in a crystal clear liquid hold out the promise of freshness—a pure, tangy, and delectable drink.

Cocktails call for a setting to match the mood. You can create this at home, by putting on Cuban music and mixing a daiquiri, for example. It is found in bars either recreated in an equally simple way or as the ultimate art form, in cases where inspired architects have modeled bars into microcosms. The latter range from London's elegant Blue Bar to the majestic Chandelier in Las Vegas; from Le Bar Long in Paris with its new communications concept to the Zebar in Shanghai, designed as a live music venue; from the M.N. Roy club, the stylized melting pot in Mexico City, to the ultra-cool, elegant Ozone Bar in Hong Kong. All of these examples are impressive, but they only really come alive through the people who frequent them. This special cocktail of elements gives these bars their unique charm, which changes from one evening to the next.

The atmosphere changes all the time, and there is a correspondingly wide range of cocktail categories to suit the mood: an inspirational Manhattan, a classic Martini or Sidecar, refreshing Highballs or Fizzes, a fruity Sangria, tropical Sunrises or Margaritas, whimsical Molecular drinks, a Bloody Mary pick-me-up, the salubrious Blackjack, heated drinks like the Vodka Sling, or a non-alcoholic "virgin" like the Mai Tai Mocktail. They cover a very wide spectrum. Matthias Stelzig, who became fascinated by the concept of mixing when still in his teens, has picked out a wide selection of recipes, though each is essential in its own way. They introduce us to the taste of the classics, encouraging us to invent our own variations. After all, the whole point in making cocktails is to conjure up spectacular drinks for ourselves and our friends, and have stylish fun in the process.

André Dominé

From al-kuhl to cocktail

The world of spirits has never been as colorful and diverse, the range on the shelves of specialist retailers and supermarkets as rich and international, or the demand for top alcoholic products as great as is the case today. Never before have the menus in bars, pubs, cafes, restaurants, and discotheques featured so many cocktails and long drinks—nor have so many bartenders in so many countries been familiar with the art of mixing, and so many private individuals taken so much pleasure in serving drinks from a shaker at home.

There is much to be learnt about the world of spirits as it has taken shape over the last 700 years or so, starting with the realization that the development of spirits is inseparable from that of medicine and culture, and of nations and societies. Ultimately, the interest in distillation had a medicinal motivation; even vermouth, bitters, and herbal liqueurs used to serve the purposes of convalescence and not indulgence.

Even back in the days of preparing medical elixirs based on distilled alcohol, the underlying principle was mixing. When enjoyment became more important, they retained the habit of making the distillate (which was often pretty rough to begin with) more palatable by adding other liquids.

The word "cocktail," the origin of which is still uncertain, entered into everyday speech in the 19th century, especially in the USA. It began as the umbrella term for short drinks made from high-proof mixtures. Now cocktail is mainly used as the generic term for all mixed drinks, even non-alcoholic creations.

Left: colored title woodcut from: Hieronymus Brunschwig, Liber de arte distillandi ("The Little Book of Distillation"), Strasbourg, 1505f.
Top: Passione, a whimsical fancy drink with Malibu, Passoa, and half a passion fruit

For a special occasion

People have always found occasion to drink. In ancient cultures alcoholic intoxication provided a gateway to the gods, this being said of the ancient Egyptians as well as the ancient Greeks, and the same is alleged of the ancient Germanic peoples. Leaving out the reason for drinking, the deciding factor was that drinking took place in company—as is the case today. Drinking alone is still viewed as questionable. As drinking has a social significance, rules were soon put in place as to who was allowed to, or had to, drink what with whom.

Initially only beer, wine, and mead were worthy of any discussion. It was only in the 18th century that drinking customs were extended to spirits, particularly home-brewed spirits. Hence farmers greeted their guests with a home brew, drinking "to their health" as, in fact, it was not that long ago that Schnapps had actually been administered as medicine.

A change in these customs came about in the 19th century with the flourishing of the economy, emerging industrialization, and spreading urbanization. This was accompanied by an increase in outlets: coffee houses and pubs, taverns, and ultimately

Edouard Manet, A Bar at the Folies-Bergère, 1881/2, London, Courtauld Institute Galleries

bars were opened—places where people met for social interaction and to enjoy a drink together.

In the Mediterranean countries, where wine had always been seen more as a foodstuff, it remains almost exclusively a food accompaniment to this day and is not normally touched outside mealtimes. When people meet prior to the midday or evening meal, it is time for an aperitif. The drinks that were initially served as such were indeed appetite stimulants, many of them containing quinine and other stimulatory plants and herbs. Even absinthe, flavored predominantly with aniseed, was largely a stimulant first and foremost.

BEFORE AND AFTER MEALS

Once the occasions became established, the producers moved on to developing drinks specifically for these occasions and even creating brands to suit them.

Today the aperitif or before-dinner drink is perhaps the most frequent of these occasions, deriving from the indispensable habit in the Mediterranean region of popping into the local bar before the midday or evening meal for a well-earned drink.

This is coupled with the worldwide custom of beginning every gathering, every party, and every celebration that usually involves a meal with at least one if not more introductory drinks. Depending on country, status, and preference, a wide variety of spirits can be served as cocktails or long drinks, or else sherry, white port, vermouth, or bitters, for example. It is not unusual for such preludes to extend over two hours. Bars, which are frequented less often before dinner, attract customers with

Pastis or other aniseed spirits remain the most popular aperitif throughout the Mediterranean region.

Happy Hours and the availability of drinks at reduced prices.

Then comes the phase after the meal, particularly the evening meal. First of all the various classics are offered as digestifs because alcohol aids digestion. This is the best moment for the great distillates, especially those that have aged for years in oak barrels, be it cognac, Armagnac, Brandy de Jerez, or Calvados, or other aged apple or plum Schnapps varieties such as vintage whiskies and rums, or well-aged tawnys, madeiras, sherrys, and banyuls.

Once night falls the stage is set for after-dinner cocktails. Thereafter it is time for the bars, clubs, or discotheques, and with them the full diversity of mixed drinks.

Fine for a time

In a well-organized bar it is the colorful liqueurs that first attract attention from among the rows of very different bottles on the shelves, today taking up more and more space, while in the end your eyes are sure to linger on the elaborate bottles and carafes indicative of expensive distillates. The order is left to the barkeeper's discretion, but he does ensure that the spirits he uses the most are the ones that are quickest to hand.

The following chapters present spirits according to their categories, relate their histories, define their methods of production, explain their differences in quality,

Attractive before-dinner drinks

and demonstrate their possible uses with the help of recipes.

The classic breakdown of spirits and cocktails served in the world of gastronomy comprises aperitifs and digestifs—i.e. before-dinner and after-dinner drinks. Spirits themselves are often subject to such different categorization that it is difficult to allocate them to the two traditional groups of aperitifs and digestifs. The most consumed alcoholic drinks today, vodka and white rum, are characterized by their largely neutral flavor, making them ideal for mixing and a range of other uses, especially in light, refreshing drinks.

Neat high proof is not suitable prior to a meal, and that is why aperitifs initially include wine-based drinks, provided—to every rule there is an exception—that they are on the dry side. Hence vermouth, dry sherries, madeiras, white ports, and marsalas fall into this category. These are joined by those members of the complex category of liqueurs that can be mixed with mineral water, soft drinks, or juices, although these are usually the bitter liqueurs. Their advantage is their quick and easy preparation.

Classic spirits such as gin, whisk(e)y, and cognac are admitted in their diluted form, most simply with soda or with other mixers in more sophisticated versions such as highballs, while the addition of lemon juice—as with gin—produces a refreshing result. The aniseed spirits play a special role, most of them being diluted with chilled water and being considered aperi-

The barkeeper—as shown here at the Green Door Bar in Berlin—is less concerned with a spirit's category than with its easy accessibility.

tifs par excellence due to their low alcohol content, their character, and the effect of the aniseed. If aperitifs are to be seen as a prelude to a good meal, then you should be sure to choose only drinks that do not compromise or anaesthetize the taste buds with too strong an aroma or too much alcohol.

As their name suggests, digestifs are intended to aid digestion, which they indeed do after a rich meal, thanks to the alcohol. The great classics in this category are of course the brandies as well as all of the brown spirits matured for a long time in barrels, be it whisk(e)y, rum, Calvados, or some marcs. However the pale,

aromatic distillates also put in an appearance here, primarily fruit Schnapps—as well as grappa and aquavit.

Herbal liqueurs and bitters maintain a fixed position under the digestifs, but this category does also include many other liqueurs ideally suited to harmonizing with the coffee served after a meal. Well-aged tawnys, amontillados, or banyuls are considered to be special digestifs whose outstanding aromas are better appreciated after rather than before the meal. Digestifs offer something for everyone's palate.

To your good health?

Alcohol is a toxin that can be fatal at a blood concentration of 0.4–0.5%. You can easily observe the strong effect of alcohol yourself as just a small glass of high-proof spirits causes perceptible changes. You feel excited, more relaxed, and you start to become talkative. Double the quantity brings about a certain euphoria that is generally considered to be pleasant. However, just 0.05% slows your reactions and can lead to the misjudgment of risks that even at this stage can compromise your fitness to drive.

If the percentage of the ethanol—the scientific name for alcohol—in your blood rises, then a lack of physical coordination, a loss of balance, a tendency to aggression, increasing loss of self-control, and therefore significantly reduced physical and mental ability are the result; vomiting, inebriation, and loss of memory follow as of 0.2%. As of 0.3% there is a risk of coma, and even death.

The way in which a person reacts to the intake of ethanol differs according to the individual and depends on a great many factors, including body weight, state of health, age, genes, and gender. Asians are less able to tolerate alcohol than western Europeans, women less than men. Anyone who has dined well on rich food can genuinely afford an extra glass. As a preventive measure, try to drink a glass of water more often between alcoholic drinks, as well as several afterwards.

Trinket keinen Branntwein, denn er ist Gift.

"Drink no brandy, for it is poison."
Colored chalk lithograph from Neuruppin Prints, around 1850

What is alcohol?

Alcohol or, scientifically, ethanol is a color-less liquid with an intense, penetrating smell. It comprises two carbon atoms, five hydrogen atoms, and a hydroxyl group. Also known colloquially as spirits, ethanol has two distinct properties: firstly it is highly inflammable and burns with a pale, blue flame, forming CO_2 and water

vapor; secondly, it is strongly water absorbent, hygroscopic, and therefore a strong, proven solvent. Ethanol is lighter than water with a density of 0.7913 g/cm^3 and vaporizes earlier with a boiling point of just above 173 °F (78.3 °C). Ethanol occurs naturally through fermentation, in which yeast converts fructose into alcohol and carbon dioxide. This occurs automatically in ripe fruit as well as in other foodstuffs. For example, bread can contain up to 0.3% vol. ethanol, sauerkraut around 0.5% vol., and a ripe banana up to 1% vol.

Even though alcohol has played a medicinal role from the earliest times through to today, having been and still being used to extract the active agents from plants in order to administer them to patients, its abuse leads to addiction and thereby to a multitude of illnesses, often followed by an early death. There are two main categories of illness: one category comprises psychic and neurological conditions such as depression and hallucinations, dementia, and epilepsy; the other comprises the consequences of metabolic problems, including cirrhosis of the liver, impotence, cardiac insufficiency, various types of cancer, and a general weakening of the immune system.

No less serious are the social problems and irresponsible behavior caused by excessive alcohol consumption, not least among teenagers and among drivers. For a number of years now the manufacturers and producers of alcoholic drinks and their industry associations have been carrying out effective consumer education, particularly among those sectors of the population at risk—especially teenagers, with concrete results starting to become apparent.

In addition, the discussion as to whether moderate alcohol consumption is beneficial to health continues. It is interesting to note that recent studies carried out among older people show that low-level alcohol consumption and a good state of health are often related.

Spirit and intellect: the distillation idea

You only need to bring water to the boil in a covered saucepan on the stove and to then remove the lid: the drops on the inside of the lid are an example of distillation. The water reaches its boiling point, rises as vapor, meets the cooler saucepan lid, and condenses to form water again. If you vaporize a mixed liquid, then the different components volatilize out of the mixture in the order of their boiling points. So much for the physical side of things. The basic prin-

Matthaeus Platearius compiled one of the key pharmaceutical works of the Middle Ages in 1150, the De medicinis simplicibus.

ciple was known to the Sumerians back in the 13th century B.C.—at least, the principle of distillation itself, not necessarily the distillation of alcohol. The first applications of this technology were for the purposes of beauty care and personal hygiene, being used to extract essential oils from plants. Once the plants are chopped up and the mixture heated in water, the water vapor "carries" the ephemeral agents with it. The oil then separates from the water in the resulting condensate—from *destillare*, meaning to drip. Around 1,000 years later Greek sailors used this principle in order to obtain drinking water from seawater while at sea, evaporating the water and collecting the condensate.

The vessels used were constantly adapted to their purpose, and the ancient Egyptians designed a cap for the rounded lower part to which a pipe was attached, from which the distillate could drip.

A COOL HEAD

The cap or helmet so important for efficient dripping was known as the *alanbiq* in Arabic, which the Romans adopted as the *alambicus*, an accepted term in many languages today. The alembic became the typical instrument of alchemists—motivated by the teachings of Aristotle—who endeavored to perfect metal and convert it into gold. Although they did not achieve

Alembics came to Andalusia with the Moors, but it was only centuries later that they were used for distilling wine. This is Gonzalez Byass' new distillery.

this, they did make numerous discoveries regarding chemical elements, substances, and processes. It was for the extraction of rose water that distillation technology was largely perfected, rose water having become a lucrative trading commodity in the Middle East after 900.

There is still one decisive prerequisite for the distilling of alcohol: the distillation of substances with boiling points lower than that of water (geraniol, the main component in rose oil, boils at 446 °F/ 230 °C, alcohol at 173 °F / 78.3 °C). In order to be able to collect them, the heating has to be done carefully and the rising vapors cooled. This realization is ascribed to the Persian alchemist Abu Musar Dschabir Ibn Hajjan, while the physician Al Razi (Abu Bakr Mohammad Ibn Zakariya al-Razi, 865–925) was the first to record how substances with low boiling points are distilled. He is also said to have distilled wine, naming the result al-kull, the whole, and to have used it for

medical treatment because of its sterilizing properties. In Arabic *al-kuhl* referred to eye makeup and it was only in Spain that the word became reinterpreted as spirits.

It was the Moors who brought alchemical skills to Europe, where alchemy, science, and philosophy underwent a significant upsurge in the 11th century. In Salerno the monks' hospital belonging to the Monte Cassino monastery became one of the first medical universities in Europe. It was here that a recipe was copied into Matthaeus Platearius' famous medicinal book *De medicinis simplicibus*, known as the *Circa instans* (after the first words of the introduction) in the mid 12th century. It contained instructions on how to produce *aqua ardens*, fire water, the common name for spirits throughout the Middle Ages. The distillation of alcohol in Europe had begun.

Remedy and indulgence

Two physicians stand at the forefront of the modern art of distilling: the Italian Taddeo Alderotti and the Spaniard Arnaldus de Villanova. Alderotti (known in his writings as Thaddaeus Florentinus, ca. 1223–1303), was born in Florence, and taught medicine at the University of Bologna from 1260, where he began distilling wine a few years later. His work *De virtutibus aquae vite et eius operationibus* provides a detailed description of how high-proof spirits can be obtained through repeated distillation. Three to four runs were usual, but at least ten were required for an especially pure distillate, the *aqua vitae perfectissima* or *rectivicata*. These rectifications were made possible by an important new development: the *canale serpentinum*, a winding pipe housed in a cooling vessel kept cold with water, in which the vapors containing the alcohol condensed. This technology became widespread among alchemists and chemists at the end of the 13th century, and both Alderotti and his colleagues recognized that this distillate was ideally suited to medicinal purposes.

One of the most famous physicians of the age was Arnaldus de Villanova (ca. 1235–1311), personal physician to the king of Aragon. He considered the *aqua vitae* to be a universal remedy, recommending its application in numerous works as well as that of a variety of flavored wines that he described in his *Liber de vinis*. While the laboriously produced *aqua vitae* was initially administered to the sick by the spoonful, an epidemic in the second half of the 14th century required a less restrained approach

At the start of the 16th century the stills were not able to exceed a certain size purely for manufacturing reasons, so several of them were heated over a heat source. (Hieronymus Brunschwig, Liber de arte distillandi de simplicibus, *Strasbourg 1505)*

to spirits. Helpless in the face of the plague and death, people placed their faith, not entirely without justification, in the strength of the water of life—often acquiring a taste for it in the process. The first commercial distilleries with large stills were established in the centuries that followed.

The Strasbourg physician Hieronymus Brunschwig (ca. 1450–1513) provided such a detailed description of distilling in his widely circulated books that people were able to reproduce the process. The use of corn mash became widespread as of the mid 16th century, making alcohol affordable and available in larger quantities. The distillation process remained largely unchanged for several centuries. In order to be able to separate as much water as possible from the alcohol, distilling had to be carried out several times, and this could only be done consecutively.

A first important further development, patented in 1801, can be attributed to the French chemist and physicist Jean-Edouard Adam (1768–1807), who arranged several vessels behind one another in which the alcohol vapors partially condensed, enabling him to produce a better yield. The decisive step toward today's column stills, however, came in 1808 from the Frenchman Jean-Baptiste Cellier-Blumenthal (1768–1840), who ran a sugar beet factory in Belgium. He was the first to use a column with several bubble cap trays on top of one another in order to concentrate the alcohol. In Scotland Robert Stein put together his still in 1826; it was perfected by the Irishman Aeneas Coffey and patented in 1831. His column device allowed for repeated, continual distilling without

An old, hand-crafted column still at Florio in Marsala

interruption in a kind of circulatory system, making it considerably more cost effective. It became the basic model not only for industrial stills but also for modern stills, with rectifier columns as used today by top-class distillers.

Old still from the historic corn distillery in Hilden, Fabry-Museum

Distillation: classic

When distilling spirits a slightly alcoholic liquid is extracted from the alcohol and collected separately. The liquid in question also has to be heated so that the alcohol, with a boiling point of 173 °F (78.3 °C), vaporizes before the water. This vapor is collected and allowed to condense, either using batch and/or coflow distillation, or by means of continual and/or counterflow distillation.

The principle behind the older, batch method is based on two aspects: on the one hand the rising alcohol vapors need to be cooled so that they then condense; on the other hand, repeated distilling is necessary in order to obtain a higher alcohol content and a purer distillate. Gener-

ations of distillers have sought to increase the efficiency of their distilling plants ever since the 13th century. The unit itself essentially comprised of an oven, with a pumpkin-shape still, and a pipe through which the rising alcohol vapors were fed off and cooled. A major improvement was the replacement of the glass still with a copper one, enabling an increase in volume. In the 15th century the next step was the placing of a helmet on top of the still with a winding spirit pipe, the swan's neck, through which the vapors slowly rose. Today we know that the shape of this helmet has a decisive influence on the character of the distillate.

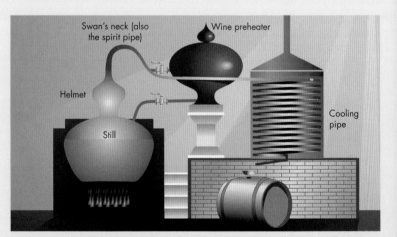

The famous model for batch distillation is the alambic charentais for cognac.

ONE AFTER THE OTHER

Distilling begins with the filling of the still. The first batch comprises wine, beer, or the alcohol-containing mash, and is usually heated by gas today. In the first run this is distilled to a still slightly cloudy raw spirit with an alcohol content of between 25 and 35% vol. (depending on the starting substance). The raw spirit also contains aromatic substances such as ester, aldehyde, various alcohols and acids such as terpene, and acetals as well as the infamous fusel oils. All of the insoluble and non-volatile components, on the other hand, remain in the still. For the second batch the distiller collects enough raw spirit in order to refill the still—but not without having cleaned it thoroughly beforehand. With a second unit the process can be continued with no time loss. The distiller requires experience and expertise for the extraction of the refined spirit. He has to raise the temperature carefully in order to use the opportunity to separate the first runnings, the first part of the condensing distillate with undesired, slightly volatile substances such as methanol. This is followed by the middle runnings or the heart: he begins with an alcohol content of up to 80% vol. that then sinks gradually during the course of distillation. Depending on the starting material, the distiller lets it sink down to 55–45% vol. before drawing off the end runnings that contain the fusel oils. The sooner the middle runnings are ended, the purer the distillate, but a small proportion of fusel oils can ensure greater complexity and more character in spirits aged in barrels for many years. The alcohol content of the refined spirit, which amounts to about one third of the quantity of raw spirit, varies between 60 and 75% vol.

Modern versions of the alambic charentais at Cognac Frapin

Distillation: modern

Batch distilling, or coflow distillation, is a complex method that is both time consuming and cost intensive, but that produces outstanding results because it enables the precise separation of the first and last runnings. Continual and/or counterflow distillation is quicker and more cost effective, producing a higher alcohol concentration, albeit at the expense of the aroma agents. The first continual distilling unit to be built was developed by the Frenchman Jean-Baptiste Cellier-Blumenthal and was patented in 1808. The Scotsman Robert Stein experimented with his notion of more rational distillation in the 1820s, a concept that was then perfected by the Irishman Aeneas Coffey as the highly complex continual patent still that was patented in 1831 and that bears his name.

The basic principle behind continual and/or counterflow distillation requires that the liquid to be distilled flows constantly and the alcohol contained therein is vaporized, condensed, and continually fed off. This occurs by means of one or several rectifier columns comprising several separating bubble cap trays functioning as small stills. The liquid is poured into the column from above and flows downward through the perforated separating layers. In the process it encounters the vapor rising from the bottom of the column that heats it, vaporizing the alcohol contained therein, so that it begins to rise. From layer to layer, condensing in part at each level and dripping down again, the alcohol leaves other liquid substances behind, becoming ever more concentrated until it reaches the condenser via the spirit pipe. The alcohol-free liquid is then fed out of the column.

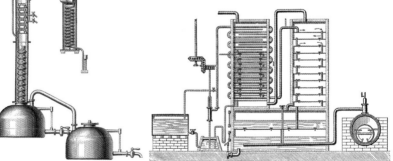

Left: The Cellier-Blumenthal apparatus (patent 1808); the wine is added from the top right. Right: Coffey's patent still (1831)

Today the majority of spirits are distilled using the continual method, be it vodka, rum, Bourbon, or grain whisk(e)y.

TOP OF THE RANGE DISTILLATION UNIT

The development of the column devices ultimately gave blacksmiths the idea of combining conventional stills with a column to enable top-class distillers to complete batch distillation in one distilling process, in which the distillate is simultaneously rectified and/or cleansed and concentrated. (The example comes from Arnold Holstein, a producer from Lake Constance in Germany specialized in distillation technology.)

The still, made from tempered copper, is filled from the side. It is heated in the water bath, which avoids any risk of scorching. An agitator is integrated for more viscous mashes.

A variety of layers can be fitted individually in the fine distillate column. Using the dephlegmator, which condenses vapors by means of targeted cooling and feeds them back into the column, the middle runnings produce a very high concentration of aroma components.

The catalyzer ensures the reduction of undesired acids. At the top of the catalyzer the vapors are fed through a pipe to the actual cooling tube, the distillate emerging from its lower end. These perfected distilling units and the fact that top-class distillers now focus on the highest quality mean that distillates of an unprecedented clarity and finesse are now being produced.

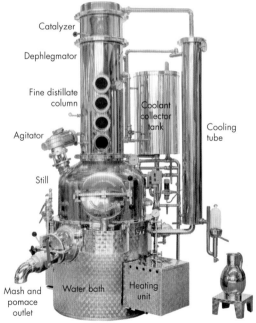

Catalyzer

Dephlegmator

Fine distillate column

Coolant collector tank

Cooling tube

Agitator

Still

Mash and pomace outlet

Water bath

Heating unit

Elixirs and profits

Once knowledge of the processes behind the technology of distillation became more widespread with the first publications about it, more and more physicians, chemists, and alchemists managed to produce colorless, slightly inflammable spirits. They did not find the philosopher's stone but they did discover the *quinta essential*, the quintessence of life. They discovered that this substance had further astounding properties aside from its flammability, particularly from a medicinal perspective. It was its decay prohibiting and disinfecting properties that made the use of pure alcohol a blessing. What's more, it absorbed the active agents from other plants in previously unknown concentrations.

However, it took an immense amount of effort to obtain just a small quantity of this water of life, and so it remained a precious panacea for a long time. It was the monasteries, in particular, that took up its production, thereby obtaining a multitude of tinctures—the predecessors of liqueurs.

SPIRITS BRING PROFITS

The consumption of spirits gradually spread throughout Europe, but remained a local affair initially until Dutch merchants discovered its benefits in the 16th century. When The Netherlands rose to become the greatest trading power in the 17th century, brandewijn became one of the most lucrative trading commodities. To start with,

The well and alembic (in background) at the Frapin estate in Cognac are testament to the centuries-old tradition.

the Dutch bought wine in the harbors of the French Atlantic coast, then sold it at home or in the Baltic countries. There were large quantities available in the Charente in particular, but the quality was poor. The Dutch merchants showed considerable interest in the distillation of wine that began there in the mid 16th century as, unlike wine, spirits were non-perishable and required only a fraction of the space for transportation. Like wine, spirits were not considered a luxury but simply as a thirst quenching drink, the crystal clear distillate being mixed with what was at that time often polluted water.

The Dutch obtained their spirits from the Cognac region, via Bayonne harbor, as well as later from Armagnac. Like wine, the spirits were transported in barrels, and it was soon discovered that this improved them and that they took on an attractive color after a while. The customers in London in particular—England was the principal brandy customer—noticed significant differences in quality depending on the origin and the type of barrel. Accordingly, toward the end of the 17th century the upper classes began to make specific demands for specific brandies, particularly the brandy from Cognac, for which they were willing to pay higher prices. This made cognac a forerunner of a development that only took hold in other regions and countries in the 19th century, namely the development of high-quality spirits.

Cellar at the Château de Salles (Armagnac)

Paradise at Hennessy (Cognac)

Everyday alcohol

The emergence of modern spirits as we know them today is inseparable from the development of western society. The Industrial Revolution was the most important factor in this process, bringing with it increased urbanization as well as completely new work and income structures. The influence of the nobility declined while the middle class—who now were able to play a decisive role in economic, political, and cultural life—grew in significance.

France provided the most striking example of these changes. Antoine Beauvilliers, former quartermaster to the counts of Provence, opened the first upmarket restaurant in Paris in 1782. A number of others followed his example but in the year of the revolution, 1789, there were not even 50 restaurants in Paris. One of the far-reaching consequences of the revolution was that the nobility's kitchen staff lost their jobs. What solution was more obvious for them than to set up a location where people could "revitalize" themselves?

As a result, by 1820 there were already some 3,000 restaurants established in Paris.

The gastronomical expansion was one prerequisite for the later success of beverage brands, but there was also another: new mealtimes. All of a sudden there was a time span in the late afternoon that was ideally suited to visiting one of the large boulevard cafes and to enjoy a drink, an aperitif.

Spirits became brands that were portrayed by famous poster artists (this one by Giorgio Muggiani) wanting to establish a name for themselves.

Even back then the modern trend showed a clear preference for addressing women.

THE THIRSTY BOURGEOISIE

The development of a well-to-do middle class brought with it potential consumers for branded beverages. At the start of the 19th century the evolution had already begun in Turin and Milan, where the drinking of vermouth was met with much enthusiasm. As the manufacturers ensured vigorous competition for one another, each of them tried to gain exposure for their brand. One example was Cinzano, taking part in the second World Exhibition in London in 1862 in order to present their own vermouth brand, and of course using the gold medal they won there as a sales pitch.

The Belle Époque era was the real boom time, with Europe not only experiencing a further wave of industrialization toward the end of the 19th century, but also a comparatively long period of peace. Cafes and coffee houses developed into society meeting places, the frequenting of which was seen as a lifestyle expression. The bars provided the scope for casual exchanges as well as giving rise to entirely now consumer behavior at the same time. People met to enjoy a drink together and the industry reacted with a constant range of new and intriguing drinks: apéritifs à base de vin, vermouth, bitters, absinthe, liqueurs. Anyone having trouble deciding between the wealth of options could refer to the new but already widespread advertising media such as calendar posters, water fountains, and placards. Branded drinks were here to stay.

Modern style

When Jerry Thomas published the world's first cocktail book in 1862 with his Bar-Tender's Guide or How to Mix Drinks, he himself was able to look back on several years' experience gained in various hotels and saloons; he had earned the nickname "Professor" not only with his artistic drinks, but also with his show-time acts. His book, which was expanded several times, presented a wealth of different drinks, thus demonstrating how widespread and how popular mixed drinks were in the United States at the time.

The cocktail's popularity actually increased during Prohibition because it served as a disguise on the one hand, and its non-alcoholic ingredients often helped to cover up the objectionable taste of the illegally brewed or smuggled fusel alcohol. This extensive source of inspiration became an enduring enrichment to the bartender's recipe repertoire.

It was with envy that the world of the 1950s viewed the Americans and their American way of life, a life in which the bar was an institution— one that subsequently spread internationally, together with the knowledge of spirits and the requisite creative skills. Even though new ones were constantly being added, recipes still focused on gin, rum, and whisk(e)y and, like the

On Vienna's Kärntner Durchgang, Adolf Loos, pioneer of modern architecture and art theorist (Ornament and Crime, 1908), designed this tiny American Bar in 1908.

legendary martini, were often bristling with alcoholic content. When vodka appeared in the 1970s as a non-communist, neutral-tasting spirit, it took over the alcohol proportion of many mixed drinks as well as gaining first place in the popularity stakes a decade later, way ahead of all its competitors.

The recipes have since become ever richer in ingredients and the world of cocktails (now the prevalent umbrella term) is all the more colorful, exotic, and playful. Modern bar patrons have "slim," "sporty," and "healthy" as their ideals and expect drinks to match. The awareness that excess alcohol is damaging to health has led to the establishment of the "less but better" trend and to an increase in demand for high-quality spirits. Distilleries with genuine tradition, distinct origins, and inspirational quality have suddenly become the focus of attention. The world of spirits has never been as fascinating as it is today.

Spirits stipulations

It goes without saying that legislators have paid detailed attention to the production and sale of spirits. Apart from the protection aimed at teenagers in particular, legislation is primarily concerned with the concept definition, designation, packaging, and labeling of spirits, as well as with the protection of geographic indications. Regulation no. 110/2008 passed by the European Parliament and the Council of Europe has been in force within the European Union since May 2008 and is available for review in the internet in all of the community's languages. "The measures applicable to the spirit drinks sector should contribute to the attainment of a high level of consumer protection, the prevention of deceptive practices and the attainment of market transparency and fair competition," says the regulation. This is not intended to oppose innovation, but the latter must serve "to improve quality, without affecting the traditional character of the spirit drinks concerned." It is emphasized that the production of spirits constitutes an important market opportunity for agricultural products from within the Community. In order to safeguard diversity the member states have the right to impose stricter regulations within their own territory. Detailed appendices to the regulation provide details of technical concept definitions and conditions, define the numerous categories, and list those spirits that may declare themselves to be of a specific geographic origin.

In the USA, the ATF—the Bureau of Alcohol, Tobacco, and Firearms and Explosives—concerns itself with these matters, and that also determines the rules governing the advertising of alcohol, in cooperation with the Federal Trade Commission.

Location bar

People have sat down, chatted, celebrated, and drunk together since time immemorial. But they didn't need taverns just for that. Merchants and pilgrims who left home for long periods were grateful to find a place where, ideally, they could not only rest their weary bones, but find sustenance to satisfy their hunger and quench their thirst when they were far from home. There was a long, if not predestined, way to go, however, before the first perfectly stirred martini. A combination of good company, exchanges of information, and the catering trade was destined for global success. We now know it by the name of "bar."

In the time of the Roman Empire relay posts where travelers could obtain provisions grew up at major crossroads. In time taverns and public houses became popular with the locals too, who would call in to such establishments even if they were not traveling through. Innkeepers became content to forego unpredictable passing trade, preferring to serve the local inhabitants. Their taprooms over the centuries would become meeting places for simple folk. Rich citizens and the higher earners—where such existed—expected more sophisticated fare in a more genteel atmosphere.

Not until the 20th century did a degree of democratization enter the trade. Many bars ceased to exclude certain sectors of the population categorically, but did deliberately appeal to specific interest groups. In the 1960s bars adapted to a wide range of different tastes started to open. There were Caribbean bars, coffee bars, singles bars, milk bars, dance bars, cigar bars, wine bars—which meant that virtually every preference was catered for.

In many bars the atmosphere is inextricably linked with the regular clientele that frequent it, forming a unique microcosm. People go to the Western bar in their cowboy outfits, the bikers' bar in leathers, and the tango bar in slightly faded elegance. When you enter such settings you leave your daily life behind you at the door. For many customers the appeal of the institutions we call bars lies in that very fact.

Left: The M.N. Roy in Mexico City is an inspired blend of different architectural styles.
Top: The Singapore Sling, made with Heering Cherry Liqueur, was invented in the bar of the Raffles Hotel.

Barely respectable

The early settlers to the North American continent didn't have it easy. They worked hard morning till evening and many families lived an isolated existence on their farms. Any shopping trip into the next "town" would have been a welcome change. The local store sold everything a settler could need and some things he didn't actually need, among them alcohol, probably whiskey, on tap. Whether such establishments took the form of general stores or drugstores is the subject of much speculation. For certain, there were as yet no bars even though the name is said to have had its origins in that era. Cautious shop owners are said to have barricaded fragile goods against vandalism from brawling alcohol consumers, hence the word "bar."

About 1800 the name "saloon" came into common use for establishments other than grocery stores that sold alcoholic drinks across the counter. It probably derives from the Italian word *salone*. Depending on the location these were initially tents or booths where whiskeys that gloried in brand names such as Tarantula Juice or Coffin Varnish were dispensed. As time went by the buildings became more robust and investments were made in the furnishings, which went from the rough and ready rustic to bour-geois and ostentatious. Their customers were almost exclusively men. No respectable woman would have been seen in a saloon.

This changed in the bars of the 19th century. Opened near to or even inside

The clients in the Wild West could be somewhat unruly, so the host had to erect a barricade (the bar is therefore actually a divider). Here cowboys in Texas stand at a bar in 1910. No respectable woman would have joined them there.

the better hotels in prosperous cities, bars quickly became the expression of a new attitude to life.

The first bar book, the Bartender's Guide, was published in 1862 by American bar keeper Jerry Thomas. In addition to rules of conduct for the bartender toward their customers, there is a handy selection of recipes. In 1869 the best barkeepers in the USA competed with one another in a mixing championship held in Chicago. By the turn of the century the bar had become a fixed point in the American way of life. In the "golden age of American drinking," according to society critic Henry Louis Mencken, the basis had been created for the fame of manhattans, martinis, old fashioneds, and cobblers, all served with ice delivered to the door, in those days, by the ice man on his horse-drawn cart.

Prohibition between 1920 and 1933 drastically restricted alcohol consumption in the USA. Substances such as hair lotion and antifreeze were used in the illicit production of spirits, and such "poison" was best mixed and diluted. Nevertheless, by the end of the dry period a fund of cocktail knowledge had been lost. American journalist Wayne Curtis joked that this had been as devastating for the American drinking culture as the burning of the library of Alexandria for the ancients.

Nowadays the "bar" is so anchored in our minds that even fictional bars such as Humphrey Bogart's, or rather Rick Blaine's, Rick's Café Américain in Casablanca are more alive to many of us than any real building in the next street. The sitcom Cheers, which made do with just a bar as a backdrop for its 11-year success story between 1982 and 1993, reaped more than two dozen Emmy awards.

Mata Hari (Greta Garbo) among her adoring fans at the Paris bar. Although the movie was set in 1914, the bar is more in the style of the period in which it was made, 1931, which also applies to the clothes of the customer in the foreground.

Old expatriate bars

Many of the now legendary first bars in Europe took their inspiration from America or benefited from American assistance. And with this American influence the myth of the bar was propagated.

Americans who in the 20th century, for whatever reasons, found themselves temporarily in the land of their forebears would find a little piece of their own culture in the bars that had grown up there, where they could feel at home. Cafes full of expatriate Americans and American bars became hot spots.

Harry's Bar in Venice, the Bar Vendôme at the Paris Ritz, and the Viennese Loos American Bar—built by genius architect and artist Adolf Loos in 1908 after travels in the United States—were small exclaves of ordinary American culture. Occupying soldiers and exiled literati, stragglers, and refugees all stopped there to experience a little piece of home and a sense of belonging. The Paris cafes, for example, were constant meeting points for so many authors and artists that expatriate Americans in Paris in the 1920s created their own literary genre.

One anecdote from the long history of Harry's Bar in Venice illustrates just how important bars were as contact points. Giuseppe Cipriani, who opened his establishment in 1931 and made a good name

Harry's Bar in Venice, opened in 1931, had many imitators.

for himself, could not always choose his customers. He served his last Bellini when the Italian fascists commandeered the bar as a canteen for naval forces. When in 1946 the Allies put an end to the specter of fascism, Cipriani was running a small hostelry on the island of Torcello off Venice. There he was summonsed by the American military command, only to be showered with reproaches. An American officer rebuked him severely, saying that he could not be a good Italian because he had not yet reopened Harry's Bar. It was only a few months later that Harry's Bar, named after Cipriani's former partner Harold Pickering, was once more an (almost) permanent institution in its location near to St. Mark's Square.

You can still enjoy a Bellini at Harry's Bar. However, the old clientele who came here to forget their foreign status temporarily are no longer to be found. Instead you will encounter tourists with colorful shorts and digital cameras, all in pursuit of a myth, a reminder of what American bars once meant to European culture. But for a furnished room with atmosphere to become a bar, you also need the right kind of people having the right kind of conversations.

Harry's New York Bar in Berlin is reminiscent of a 1970s style bar.

Exotically seductive

With its spices, fabrics, and teas, South East Asia has long been a major trading destination for European merchants. But the route there was long and arduous, and daily life in the hot, humid tropics was strange and stressful. How refreshing to escape the hurrying throngs and the rickshaw drivers threading their way through the crowds, to enjoy a cool, reviving drink in a quiet atmosphere.

Bars grew up from India to China as consoling refuges. Their clients were thousands of miles from home, in the middle of a culture the customs and habits of which were almost as incomprehensible to them as the languages spoken.

This distancing was quite helpful in staving off the sense of culture shock. Where could it be more pleasantly conquered than in a bar that was a mixture of the best of several civilizations: colonial tastefulness and British character with exotic foods and beverages. The colonial style—with its rattan chairs, carved furniture, and hunting trophies such as elephant tusks—could hardly find a more suitable setting than in the Far Eastern hotel bars.

Some of them earned their reputation for more than just catering. When the Raffles Hotel in Singapore—named after Sir Thomas Stamford Raffles, founder of the new Singapore—opened its doors for the

The Long Bar of the Raffles Hotel, where the Singapore Sling (p. 120) was invented.

The Ara Bar in the Taj Tashi Hotel in Bhutan (left) and the bar of Raffles in Dubai (right) are exclusive venues.

first time on December 1, 1887, 1 Beach Road immediately became one of the top addresses in the city and the establishment's fame rose just as steadily as the number of its building extensions.

The hotel was acclaimed too for its Long Bar. Some time between 1910 and 1915, the first Singapore Sling was mixed. Whatever the Singapore Sling contains—and whatever it costs—knowing that you are drinking it in the Long Bar of the Raffles where it was first created may well increase its thrill. Many illustrious clients at this hotel have savored its delights, among them Charlie Chaplin and Jean Harlow, representatives of the old Hollywood, and George Bush Senior and Rudy Giuliani,

representatives of the late 20th-century political scene. But the Raffles isn't just a showcase for personal dramas. Dramas of a theatrical kind have taken place there too. Short stories and movies have been set at the Raffles. Joseph Conrad and Rudyard Kipling, who both spent a large portion of their lives in South East Asia, put up here. They incorporated their experiences at the Raffles into their works, sometimes written while actually staying at the hotel. For Somerset Maugham, the influential author and chronicler of the end of the colonial period in South East Asia, the Raffles became a symbol of "all the fables of the exotic East."

Unmistakably

Pirates, smugglers, and Englishmen have all had a significant influence on Cuba's history. All had designs on the favorable harbor and the legendary treasures of what is now Cuba's capital. And they all drank rum. Lots of rum. Together with the slave trade, rum was long a major cornerstone of the infamous trade triangle between the Caribbean, Africa, Europe, and North America.

Havana's harbor districts have seethed with life for centuries. Seafarers and travelers were hungry for entertainment and the landlords could always count on a steady stream of customers. In 1817 an initially unimpressive new establishment was added. The Piña de Plata soon renamed itself the La Florida and finally La Floridita. This old harborside pub is now approaching its 200th anniversary and it maintains its own web page.

Strictly speaking it owes its enduring fame to a vexation. It seems that in 1932 a young writer named Ernest Hemingway was finding it hard to cope with his new-found fame. After the success of *Death in the Afternoon*, he could hardly escape well-meaning visits by friends and those who would have liked to be his friends to his house on Whitehead Street, Key West, Florida. The solitary leisure essential to a writer was gone.

Without further ado he took the ferry to neighboring Havana and rented some quiet rooms there. In the creative peace of the fourth floor of the Ambos Mundos, he quickly started a new literary project. His work went so well that he was able to explore the district in the afternoons. Apart from deep sea fishing, he was attracted to the bars.

The Floridita proudly calls itself the birthplace of the daiquiri as here its barkeeper Constante once mixed a high-proof Special for Ernest Hemingway.

Cuban

Prohibition in the neighboring USA had guaranteed the city a constant stream of tourists for the past 12 years. Thirsty gringos landed on the island in droves, eager for a drink. Rum, which since the old colonial days had scraped a shadowy existence in the USA, became a society drink.

Hemingway, in the well-run bars of the old harbor city, discovered a love for daiquiris which he enjoyed most in the Floridita. The atmosphere of the bar and the care that his favorite bartender Constante devoted to his work fascinated him. Hemingway would later also become famous for his alcoholic escapades, and his favorite bars—the Floridita and La Bodeguita del Medio—have become destinations of pilgrimage. Nowadays literati and cocktail fans alike pay painfully high prices there, but in the alleys of the neoclassical old quarter of Havana, a World Cultural Heritage site, there are plenty of other bars and good rum—as indeed there are throughout the Caribbean.

Hemingway had his favorite bars in which to drink mojitos or daiquiris, as documented here in La Bodeguita del Medio.

An essential feature of the Havana bars are the cigars no less appreciated by Cuban women than by the aficionados.

Obviously famous

There are bars that bear his name and bars that sport his bust. He made some famous with his preferences for drinks, others into tourist attractions—such as Sloppy Joe's bar in Key West. At least one cocktail bearing his name has a fixed place in bar books and on bar lists. Of all the stars that have drunk at bars, Ernest Hemingway has certainly exerted the most influence on bar culture, being both an enthusiastic and reckless drinker. But he was not the only one.

In particular in the first half of the 20th century men of letters were accustomed to lingering in bars because at this time cafes and bars were vital artistic meeting points. Here creative people could converse and exchange ideas and inspiration with their own kind. William Faulkner, F. Scott Fitzgerald, John Steinbeck, Jack Kerouac, and Malcolm Lowry, or Dylan Thomas and Eugene O'Neill, not only wrote about alcohol, but were under its influence.

At the forefront of these was Charles Bukowski, who regarded alcohol as a means of research (which brought him to the edge of self-dissolution). Bukowski's uncompromising drinking behavior was immortalized in the 1987 movie Barfly, for which Bukowski himself wrote the script. Mickey Rourke played the role of Henri Chinaski. And Bukowski "signed" the film with a walk-on part as an aging drinker.

Countless musicians—not just obliging pianists—garnered their first stage experience in bars. Perhaps some of them for that very reason felt most at home there when

Hemingway in 1954 with Spencer Tracy, his wife, and friends in La Floridita in Havana

they were long famous and filling concert halls. Perhaps however it is because of the type of music associated with bars. In particular jazz is so closely related to bar culture that the borderline between bar and jazz club is often a very fluid one. However seldom have bars stamped the lives and work of any musician so lastingly as was the case with Tom Waits. At the beginning of his career he scraped a living performing in shabby bars and in his songs from the 1970s he repeatedly sings of social outcasts, whose ways inevitably lead to bars—not scene bars of the jet set, but gathering places of the hopeless.

For actors too bars become a stage. If they are famous they can expect, even in the gloomiest establishment, to have their every movements recorded by press and fans. And it is usually the embarrassing moments that fill the pages of the scandal sheets. And yet when stars from Liz Taylor through Paris Hilton suffer such disasters, there is always the hint of a suspicion that they have been merely carefully calculated stunts in an undignified game of publicity.

Humphrey Bogart's most famous role was largely played out in Rick's Café Américain in Casablanca. The portrayal of a man whose disappointment turns him into a cynic, but who in the end stands by his ideals, made him immortal. In real life as well Bogart spent a lot of time in restaurants and bars without ever achieving the outward serenity of Rick Blaine. "Up to half-past eleven at night he was completely normal," the owner of his favorite bar once described him, "but then he would start to think he was Humphrey Bogart."

In the movie Casablanca Humphrey Bogart played the owner of Rick's Café Américain, where expatriates and displaced persons meet. Bogart was also frequently to be found in bars in his own private life.

Chic bars

The first bars focused only on selling alcohol. But the more time the clients had on their hands, the more important inviting surroundings became. Bar owners soon realized that alcoholic drink was seldom a sufficient attraction by itself to encourage customers to come back. The staff played a vital part, as did the decor, especially if a competitor had invested in furniture, decoration, and ambience. Finally these three aspects had to fit together. Entertainment, atmosphere, and enticing drinks together would have to give the customer sufficient reason to return. The right clientele in many bars constitute an added attraction in their own right, and also, so to speak, a living asset.

To gain customers' favor bartenders strove for perfection in two respects. Barmen began to offer increasingly better drinks from ever more exotic ingredients, and interiors became ever more luxurious. This applied in particular to the magnificent American bars of the 19th century and their successors in the Old World. In large hotels the elegant bar became an object of prestige. Often it not only matches the house style, but consciously accentuates it; and occasionally it can create a deliberate counterpoint, in a style that could be elegant, undercooled, theatrical, futuristic, or intimate.

In luxury London hotel The Berkeley, the designer David Collins created the Blue Bar and made the breathtaking blue color a focal feature.

Ever changing bars

Underground bars of the 1970s and 1980s turned their backs on design mania. Famous addresses such as Studio 54 in New York, the London Ministry of Sound, and countless punk clubs of later years demonstrably denied the question of decor and set new trends. The minimalist modern bars of today have developed this heritage still further.

Bars soon began to be created around the desires of a particular clientele. The now typical form with musical entertainment was largely a product of Prohibition, when illegal speakeasies made efforts to distract attention from prohibited spirits with beautiful sounds. Particularly after World War ll, clubs became established in which music was a major factor, although this tended to be recorded rather than live. The first were known as discotheques.

Bars and clubs—the borderline between these has always been a fluid one—are no longer places of entertainment serving a single purpose. The classic American bar, living off its tranquility and expensive handmade cocktails, has more or less died out. Multifunctional establishments have replaced them, serving morning breakfast and turning themselves into lounges in the afternoon and dance clubs in the

Still a model for an adaptable and attractive bar: Bernard Khoury's B018 in Beirut

evening. Bernard Khoury perfected this concept in the B018. The tables in this Beirut club can be turned into dance surfaces. The underground bunker becomes an open-air dance floor with a retractable roof. The bar, the counter that was once a necessary barricade, is still there. But at the bar at times cappuccinos are ordered, then aperitifs and light meals, as well as tropical drinks throughout the night.

The hotel bar is now in a category of its own. It has almost lost its previous significance, but some remarkable examples do exist because hoteliers consider the bar to be part of their overall concept. Designer Philippe Starck has been doing some pioneering work in this field from Mexico to Moscow. Bars create a select ambience which in many cases is one of their main purposes. Design dominated bars do not strive after gastronomic values such as coziness, rapid service, or a private atmosphere. Design is often placed above function. And some are deliberately nothing but design.

The facilities represent both leisure area and stage setting at the same time. Philippe Starck used this concept in his designs, treating the clients as actors. He created hotels and bars that are not only somewhere to stay at the place of one's destination, but the destination itself.

ZEBAR in Shanghai was digitally designed as a "live bar" by Architects 3GATTI.

Cool and clinical

The terrace of the Ozone Bar in the Ritz Carlton, one of Hong Kong's coolest locations, overlooks Victoria Harbour—good for more than just a breath of fresh air.

Top: The flagship Icebar by Icehotel in London, where everything is made from ice from Northern Sweden. Bottom: Ozone, the highest bar in the world, has an invigorating atmosphere inside as well.

Highly approachable

Top: Il Bar of the Bulgari Hotel, London, an elegant work of art by Italian craftsmen
Bottom: grandiose staging, The Chandelier Bar in the Cosmopolitan of Las Vegas

The M.N.Roy in Mexico City is a spatialized cocktail by architects Emmanuel Picault and Ludwig Godefroy.

Philippe Starck's bars

Without him the international bar scene would be missing some of its most thrilling and original creations. Philippe Starck is arguably the most influential and imaginative designer of our times. The pioneer of democratic design and architecture, he is actively involved in the economic, ecological and technological development of his creative work. The benefits of this creativity extend to practically every sphere of life, as can be seen from his invisible micro wind turbines or the Miss Sissi lamp made from biodegradable bioplastics.

From La Main Bleue discotheque in Montreuil (1976) to the theatrical Oyster Bar of the Lan in Beijing, with its Meteorite-finish counter, Phillippe Starck has always stressed that "Freedom is the only style". The design of Le Bar Long in the Royal Monceau, Paris, encourages its guests to behave in a way that is different, and freer. Starck also applied this philosophy to the fifth Mama Shelter in Bordeaux: "Mama Shelter is the freedom, the meeting, the intelligence, the construction, the sensuality … affordable for all …".

Le Bar Long in the Royal Monceau, Paris (2010)

Top: Mama Shelter in Bordeaux (2013); bottom: The Oyster Bar in the Lan Club, Beijing (2006)

Behind the bar

There is a certain appeal in swapping sides of the bar.
Even Tom Cruise succumbed to this fascination when he
dabbled with using a shaker himself in the 1988 movie
Cocktail. Many dry, and not so dry, runs were needed for
him to master all the right moves, which he finally managed by the end of it. It is hardly surprising, for extensive
lines of bottles are stacked up behind a bartender. Profes-
sionals often have a few hundred ingredients on hand to
create more and more new drinks, not to mention exotic
juices and fresh fruit on the counter. The perfectionists
spice up their concoctions with all sorts of added extras,
finishing up with fruit.

And that is not all. The bartender spends nights on end listening. As long as he is
behind the bar, he is there for the folk in front of it, knowing what they need and when
they have had enough—of speaking and of drinking. In lively Caribbean bars especially,
any number of people are thrown together in a mood for celebration. But the party can
only go on if everyone is still on their feet. Any bartender who watches while his guests
get excessively drunk is doomed to failure.

Seasoned pros know that the job of bartender takes heart and soul. It is more a way
of life than of earning a living. Given such sheer passion, it is debatable whether a practical budget version is an option. At least it seems to involve as much work as it does
startup capital. Yet when seen in the cold light of day, the bartender's job is not really
that complicated, provided a few basic concepts are mastered.

In most mixed drinks, especially the immortal classics we know and love, a single spirit dominates. Often whole families of cocktails are named after this base drink.
So, for example, a Red, White, Black, or Green Russian owes its "national affiliation"
to vodka in each case. Coordinated liqueurs, juices, and sodas are then matched up to
each spirit. From that point on it becomes just a question of personal taste, so individual creativity can be liberally applied.

Left: Manhattan and Gin Fizz are bar classics.
Top: The Caribbean Blue, made with white rum and blue curaçao, is always a visual treat.

Getting started

By far the most important basics with a high alcohol content are whisk(e)y, gin, white rum, and vodka. While the last two of these have been rising in popularity for years, whisk(e)y and gin have been fighting against their association with open fires and graying temples. Another reason lies perhaps in the fact that they are mainly found in dry classics like Manhattans and martinis. Nearly all the popular exotic drinks that contain a high proportion of fruit are now based on vodka and rum, or their close relatives cachaça and tequila.

To start then, the four strong basics will suffice. Those with particular preferences and those who perhaps prefer fruity or sweet cocktails can manage quite well with just rum and vodka.

All that is missing are lower alcohol drinks that change the taste. These are known as "modifiers," such as vermouth which slightly varies the taste; "flavorings"

intervene more obviously in the taste profile, even though angostura bitters and grenadine are only added in small amounts. The choice of syrups is amazing.

The rest of the selection is alcohol free, meaning that it does not always have a long shelf life. For this reason, it is best always to let your own palate guide you. Ginger ale, bitter lemon, and mineral water are very good for storing. A lot of drinks stand or fall, however, with juices made from passion fruit, peach, or pineapple. It is then a matter of setting priorities. Lemons, limes, and oranges should always be in the house, for adding to the shaker really freshly squeezed.

So much for the software: now a little about the hardware, without which even the best Canadian whisky will not make a good Manhattan. The bartender's main tool is the shaker, a two-part beaker for shaking that holds whatever is appropriate for the drink. Liquids are measured using a bar measure. Stronger components are apportioned with a bar spoon, which is shaped like a long-handled teaspoon. A citrus juicer

is in almost permanent use, and for this reason an electric one is best. Fruits and peels for garnishing need to be cut with a sharp knife on a plastic chopping board.

Ice raises the next logistical problem. Firstly, how much: an ice-cube tray from the freezer compartment will not go very far. A generous supply of very cold ice must always be on hand, so a complete drawer in the freezer devoted to ice cubes is a minimum requirement. The ultimate, but expensive, next step up would be an ice-making machine.

Fast cooled by expert shaking, the finished drink flows through a special bar strainer into the appropriate glass. A few basic shapes should be available as its visual appearance is the making of every cocktail. A Bronx cuts quite a figure in a simple cocktail glass, and a Sazerac tastes different when drunk from a lovely rocks glass than from an empty mustard jar.

All in all, a touch of style does no harm. Even the trendiest cocktail is killed by empty potato chip packets and dirty plates. By contrast, an elegant tray can provide a fitting entrance for cocktail glasses. And anyone who wants to perform it all in perfect sequence must not lose hope: bar schools now offer the self-taught bartender exhaustive training camps.

This impressive range should not cause alarm, as it can all be acquired gradually.

The tools of

FOR OPENING

A crown bottle opener (7) should either sit comfortably in the hand or be fixed to the wall with a catch tray under it. At peak times this saves valuable seconds. A corkscrew must always be on hand as well. Many bar workers swear by the waiter's friend (2) with autofoiler. Longer corks can be pulled easily with a two-stage model such as the one illustrated. An additional foil cutter is another practical item (1). Champagne tongs (6) remove the wire from sparkling wine first of all, before helping to twist the cork out with leverage. And a can opener is an absolute must (5).

FOR POURING AND FOR CLOSING

Bottles that the bartender reaches for dozens of times, night after night, in order to measure out small amounts require a pourer (3). Opened bottles of wine and sparkling wine can be sealed with thick stoppers (8). The shelf life of still wines can be extended by using a vacuum pump (4) to remove the air from the partially empty bottle.

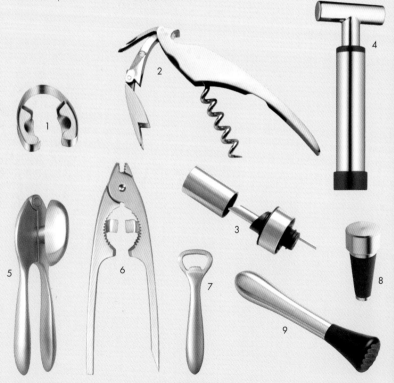

the trade

CITRUS JUICER AND MUDDLER

Fresh citrus fruits make the difference in many drinks. Squeezing by hand is a laborious business and will result in impatient customers. An electric citrus juicer (14) is a mainstay, and it should be a sturdy model with a powerful motor, capable of withstanding heavy use. The moving parts at least should be metal and easy to clean; otherwise holdups are bound to occur. Mashing is the next activity for a bartender: the most important tool for making a caipirinha is a muddler (9).

SWIZZLE STICKS, PICKS, ETC.

A set of little helpers is essential for the final finishing touches. Drinks that are to be mixed directly in the glass can be swirled (13) or stirred (11). Picks (10) and cocktail forks (12) are responsible for holding the decorations perfectly in place.

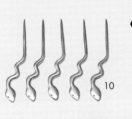

Measuring out

MEASURING

In bars not only are the measuring units regulated by law, but the proportions must be correct. For this purpose, calibrated bar measures are used for fluid ounces (fl. oz; 9) or for centiliters (cl; 8, 4). 1 US fl. oz = 29.5 cm³. Larger amounts are measured in the shaker glass (5), while the long-handled bar spoon measuring about 1/5 oz (0.5 cl) is used for smaller quantities (10), when it is not stirring, swirling, or crushing. With a twisted stem and a scoop on the end, it can be turned over to layer spirits neatly into the serving glass. For dashes and drops there are special bar bottles with fine pourers (1, 3).

CHILLING AND STIRRING

Ice is scooped (12) out of a machine or a separate bucket (7). Larger quantities of liquid are mixed in a measuring jug with pouring spout (2). Some drinks are only stirred in the shaker glass (5)—for example the classic Vodka Martini, which has regrettably been shaken, not stirred, by generations of James Bonds.

SHAKING

An indispensable tool for the bartender is a shaker with a separate strainer. This container is used to create the majority of classic drinks. And it is without doubt the most stylish way to make a mixed drink. The Boston shaker (5, 6) consists of an adjustable stainless steel beaker and a mixing glass, preferably with a measuring scale. The ingredients are put into the glass part, and then both halves are clicked together to make one tight container that is reopened by giving it a light tap on the edge of the work surface. The finished drink is then poured out of the metal beaker through a Hawthorn strainer (11), which fits several sizes of openings, and into the prepared glass. All parts can be cleaned without (almost) any effort.

Mixing and

ELECTRIC COCKTAIL MIXERS

The measuring beaker can be clasped firmly onto the mixer (1), and as it is going through the beating or fast-whipping functions the bartender can be getting on with the next task. This makes his job much easier. Thick drinks with a milk component, which are based on milk-shake recipes, are whipped up in an electric cocktail mixer. It is a traditional part of American cocktail culture.

ELECTRIC BLENDERS

The electric blender (2, 4) is a kind of multipurpose tool for the bartender. The specially shaped, stainless steel blades not only puree any type of fruit, but also even chop ice into a homogeneous mass. Smoothies and frozen drinks like Strawberry Margaritas, with their puree-style consistency, would be unthinkable without this equipment. Good blenders are heavy in order to stand up to the powerful mixing. A good motor achieves 20,000 rotations per minute and must be able to run for several minutes at the high-speed setting without damage. It is not worth having more than two different speeds and a pulse action to allow the motor to stop and start repeatedly. Professional machines turn off automatically when the

1

2

shaking

lid disengages. The special shape of the jug with cloverleaf grooves constantly channels the contents evenly down to the blades. The electric blender is a classic mainstay of the American bar, but its design makes it great for use anywhere.

HAND-HELD MIXERS

Basically a hand-held mixer (3) fulfills the same functions as the electric blender, but can also be used directly in a glass. Modern versions are impressive and powerful, but never cut ingredients quite as evenly as the electric blender's blades.

ALL-IN-ONE PROCESSORS

An expensive, but efficient, solution for small bars and personal use is the all-in-one processor (4). Within one space-saving single item are a citrus juicer, blender, and "shaver" (for fine slices and shaved ice). The motor driving all three parts is extremely powerful, producing a higher yield from squeezed oranges, faster crushed ice, and silky smooth frozen drinks. The metal rod beside the beaker is a safety feature to allow the mixer to run unattended. If it loses electrical contact with the lid, the cutting mechanism automatically shuts down.

3

4

Glasses

A bar needs a wide range of different glasses, as nearly every drink more or less matches up with a specific type of glass.

Cocktails and many short drinks are served in stem glasses (2, 3, 4, 8), and champagne-based drinks in long-stemmed flutes (6).

Fancy drinks require a pretty glass (10), usually footed and with a welled or flower-shape goblet.

Some drinks look good in red (5) and white (7) wine glasses.

Long drinks are presented in tall, straight glasses (11) or an Old Fashioned glass (12).

Tumblers (13) are good for medium drinks and for Bourbon on ice.

Malt whiskies and spirits like cognac, Armagnac, other brandies, and Calvados are sipped from a cordial glass (1), a bit bigger than a sherry glass (8).

Tall, slim glasses (9) are the classic glasses for sours.

Heat-resistant beakers (14) are for hot drinks.

Shot glasses (15) mean rapid consumption of the contents.

Glasses should always match the style of the bar as well. In a Caribbean bar ones with brightly colored stems are called for, while an exclusive hotel bar prefers to use crystal.

Ice for the bar

Accounts dating back to the 17th century exist of the summer use of naturally frozen water kept in specially constructed cold cellars. Then, in the 19th century, ice cupboards in middle class kitchens were more manageable: well-insulated cupboards for bars of ice which the iceman brought to the house entrance by horse-drawn cart on a regular basis. The USA was the first country to chill on a grand scale, firstly without and then with electricity. Electrically operated refrigerators became widespread in households in the early 20th century. The first ice-cube trays for freezer compartments appeared in the 1920s, making ice-cold drinks a permanent feature of life, as they still are today.

Although they are referred to as "cubes," the cooling elements rarely drop into the glass in the same shape and size. Squares, spheres, and cylinders, usually hollowed out on one of the flat sides, are the shapes most widely encountered. The scooped-out form originates from industrial production, where ice cubes are frozen from inside outward over cooling pins. At the end of the process the rods are briefly heated and the clear piece of ice drops off. Relatively clear ice is also produced by slowly chilling boiled water. In a refrigerator ice cubes freeze quickly from the outside inward, thus incorporating microscopic gas bubbles. This makes the cubes cloudy, and when they melt limestone sediment can be seen floating about—harmless, but unsightly.

In chemical terms ice cubes do not chill their environment, but instead draw its heat. They use this to release hydrogen bridges and assume liquid form. The energy needs associated with this process depend on the temperature of the ice cube. At 4 °F (–20 °C) it chills more effectively than a cube of the same size that is also frozen, but only at 30 °F (–1 °C).

Large ice cubes chill for longer, so they are found in long drinks. The bigger the ice surface, the faster the liquid will become cold. Crushed ice cools more quickly than an ice cube. Cobbler or shaved ice, produced mechanically, is even finer. As a general rule, 5–7 oz (150–200 g) of ice cubes should be allowed for

each drink, aiming for the upper limit if using crushed ice. In order to chill larger quantities of bottles, calculate 66–132 lb (30–60 kg) of ice in a bathtub.

Dry ice is the coldest form of ice at –108 °F (–78 °C). Dry ice is pure, solid carbon dioxide and is unsuitable for chilling in a bar, but is excellent for creating "fog" effects.

Long blocks of ice, like those used in the old ice cupboards, make fancy decorations when used for walls and counters. Colored ice cubes and ice glasses can also be introduced as gimmicks with a wow factor. Fruits and leaves can be frozen into cubes, as well as colorful ice cubes made from fruit juices.

An ice-making machine is a must for the professional bar. The bartender can then help himself using ice tongs or an ice shovel. Never the hands! Ice cubes are a foodstuff, yet tests in the catering trade have regularly revealed significant levels of bacteria such as E. coli and strepto-cocci in them. For this reason in the US they prefer to use prefilled one-way ice containers, while in India ice cubes are seen as a health risk.

For ice that has stuck together there are ice picks—reduced to small pieces it makes its way into vacuum-insulated ice buckets or champagne coolers.

Large and angular, round and hollow, crushed or shaved: all ice is not the same. An ice crusher like the one illustrated on the left involves a lot of manual labor, but is reliable. By contrast, readymade crushed ice is usually too fine: it cools things down quickly, but does not last long enough.

Fruit juices

Fruit juices—that is, drinks that come under the category of "mixers"—constitute by far the largest ingredient in many mixed drinks. As well as their ubiquitous sweetness, they give the drink the fruity taste component that often integrates with the alcoholic strength of the spirits. The perfect balance between juice and alcohol is achieved when the fruity flavors are strengthened by the alcohol, while the taste of the alcohol is tempered. A Screwdriver is a clear example of this: mixed to perfec-

tion, the vodka and orange taste distinctly better together than they do individually.

Given their importance, it is evident that the fruit juices used should be top quality, though the huge variation makes it a risky business. In the case of orange juice, the quality ranges from 100% fruit content to 6% in "fruit drink" in a carton. Pure fruit juice consists of 100% fruit, but may sometimes contain additional sweetening, even in so-called "natural" juice. Many juices are vacuum evaporated in

the country of origin, removing 50–80% of the liquid to minimize transportation costs. The concentrate is then watered down at a later stage, and is called "fruit juice made from concentrates." "Freshly squeezed juice" is pasteurized, frozen, defrosted, and pasteurized once again, making it at best a relatively fresh product.

"Nectars" contain a proportion of 25–50% fruit, depending on the type. Down at the bottom of the proportion list are the "fruit juice drinks," which are made from bottled water and sugar, with added fruit juice, composite or concentrate, giving it a fruit content of between 6% and 30%.

As many types of fruit do not contain much liquid, they appear in stores only as lightly concentrated juice in the form of nectar. Hence extracts from bananas or passion fruits have to be liberally topped up with water. With nectars up to 20% sugar may also be added, which barely conceals the poor quality of cheaper juices and adulterates every mixed drink. Juices from fruits that are high in acidity, like pineapple, are turned into dull candy water by adding sugar. Pineapple juice should only be allowed in the bar in unsweetened form.

The most sensible thing to do is to pay a visit to a delicatessen, a health food

store, or an organic store. There you will find some juices that do not contain any fruit at all. Tomato juice is the reviving ingredient in the hangover cure Bloody Mary. Here too, a high proportion of fruit or vegetable is important. Presalted or spiced vegetable juices nearly always mask poor quality. Purists use high-grade bottled tomatoes and puree them in a blender.

Even in the case of common fruits like oranges, the premium quality juices are, justifiably, very expensive. The bartender should always compare the price with an equivalent amount of fresh oranges. The better the juice is, the smaller the difference in price. In season, freshly squeezed orange juice can even be cheaper than bought juice, and it is invariably better.

An intensely fruity taste is the real kick in many mixed drinks. High-quality or freshly squeezed juice, especially from exotic fruits, can transform a simple combination into an unforgettable mixed drink. Citrus juices are absolute essentials for the bar. Their acidity gives the majority of mixtures the initial, vital freshness. The strikingly distinctive flavor of passion fruit juice puts the "good taste" into recipes like a Hurricane.

EXOTICS

Exotics such as pineapple, mango, and papaya are intensely fruity and give many tropical drinks their complex aroma. As they go well with many spirits—especially rum, tequila, and vodka—they are perfect for experimenting with new combinations. The more common, local fruits should not be ignored, however. As well as their fruity taste, peaches and apricots add a velvety consistency that gives many drinks their elegant texture. Some of these fruits take a lot of squeezing with juicers. With readymade products the fruit content is the decisive factor.

BERRIES

Juice from berries, such as blackcurrants, adds a characteristic note to many drinks. White grape juice replaces wine in non-alcoholic drinks, and even in alcoholic ones it would often have been a better choice with its rounded, grape flavor. Grapes go equally well with tropical and common fruits such as cherries.

Soft drinks and waters

Soft drinks and carbonated waters have always been ingredients in a mixed drink. They are usually one or two, or three at most, components, as in gin and tonic, where they also appear in the name of the drink itself and make it a long drink.

Nearly all soft drinks are made of flavored water, a lot of sugar, and carbon dioxide, and sometimes enhanced with drugs like quinine and caffeine. A German, Johann Jacob Schweppe, patented a process in 1783 that made it possible to carbonate water.

Not long after, Schweppes soda water began its unexpectedly meteoric career. Schweppes is also responsible for the ingenious idea of transforming quinine, the bitter malaria medicine, into a pleasant drink

called tonic water by adding sugar, lemon juice, and soda water: it was administered to British soldiers in India in the 1870s as quinine could be used in malaria prevention at this concentration. Military personnel had to swig it back on a daily basis as protection against the inevitable scurvy of sailors and the many infections encountered in occupied tropical zones.

Left: Johann Jacob Schweppe (1740–1821)

Right: John Stith Pemberton (1831–1888)

To be completely effective these beverages had a considerably higher proportion of quinine in those days. The bitter taste was correspondingly powerful, so additives to take the edge off were advisable. It is no real surprise that in classics—like highballs with ginger ale, or vodka with bitter lemon—many of the original active ingredients have been immortalized. At any rate, it is conceivable that the cocktail culture graduated from its pilot stage onboard warships.

Around the same time as the introduction of tonic water, Schweppes also incorporated ginger ale into its range, though the ginger soda only reached the peak of its popularity in the mid 20th century. By this time Coca-Cola had long since become part of the American way of life, even though the cocaine of the original recipe—brewed by the apothecary John Stith Pemberton in 1886 in the hope of overcoming his morphine addiction—was no longer in evidence.

In contrast to sodas, mineral waters are mostly neutral in flavor, and this means they do not date. Often they assume the role of the subservient vehicle for carbon dioxide. Cocktail families like Collinses, fizzes, and highballs are mainly defined by water and, not without reason, mineral water is still known as Club Soda to this day. Water has, however, established itself as a serious soft drink, so any good bar should offer a range of qualities, both sparkling and still. A well-appointed water list can prevent abstainers from alcohol from seeming like party poopers too early in the evening.

In the past ten years new readymade soft drinks and juices have kept appearing on the market, only to disappear just as quickly. Perhaps this is why hardly any of them have made it onto the ingredient list of any fashionable mixed drink. Even Sprite, which was developed in the 1960s, can only be ordered in a bar au naturel. Mixologists prefer to rely on the classics.

Sugar, syrup, etc.

Sugar is found in almost every mixed drink. On the one hand it softens the harshness of the alcohol, and on the other it takes the edge off the acidity of many fruit juices. In its natural form it is usually processed as powdered or granulated sugar—the finer it is, of course, the faster it dissolves when cold. For the traditional ritual involved in an absinthe, it has to be a sugar cube. Unrefined cane and palm sugars add their own particular note, which is eminently suited to tropical drinks. Normally the sugar is dissolved in water in advance however, and then used in liquid form. Bartenders often produce this "sugar syrup" themselves, giving them control of the sugar concentration.

Whether in the bar or at home, syrups have a special significance, most notably simple sugar syrup made from sugar cane, which gives drinks with young rum their sweetness without affecting the clarity. Even in cases where only a hint of added sweetness is required, it is indispensable.

SUGAR SYRUP, OR INVERTED SUGAR

Sugar that is heated with water to 216 °F (102 °C) and boiled for 2 minutes is known as inverted sugar. As it is heated the sugar solution begins to foam up, allowing any impurities to be removed with the foam. Usually the sugar and water are mixed in a 1:1 solution, but the proportion of sugar can be higher. The higher the sugar content, the better the preservative qualities, but the sugar is then prone to crystallization as the solution cools. To prevent this happening, up to 3/100 oz (1 g) of citric or ascorbic acid is added, causing the sucrose to split into the simple sugars glucose and fructose. The solution is heated to 167 °F (75 °C) and maintained at this tempera-

ture for up to 90 minutes, then strained into bottles. Sugar syrup can be used in any application where the texture of sugar crystals would be inappropriate.

SYRUPS

Fruit syrups provide a variety of additional flavors. A classic is grenadine, which was originally made from pomegranates but now contains only traces of the original main ingredient and all sorts of other flavorings instead. As a rule not all syrups are as natural as they seem, and their fruit content fluctuates between 10% and 38%. Some of the standard selection in the bar include strawberry, raspberry, orgeat (made from almonds), and coconut syrups, as well as Rose's Lemon and Lime juice. The product range of syrups has expanded enormously with the trend toward flavored coffees and the new-found popularity of tropical drinks. Fancy tastes are now catered for in products featuring sea buckthorn, elderflower, hazelnut, and sangria. The combination possibilities for mixed drinks are far from exhausted yet, so look out for more to come.

MILK, CREAM, EGGS, AND ICE CREAM

Flips, eggnogs, and coffee-based drinks require milk products. In modern versions of coladas the coconut taste is refined with cream. Many syrups go well with milk. And of course milk, cream, eggs, and ice cream form the basis of non-alcoholic drinks like milk shakes. These ingredients, with the exception of ice cream, are relatively perishable, so for this reason many bars stock long-life milks and cream. Pity the cocktails made with them. High-grade fresh milk lasts longer than you might think, as does cream, and they can make an ordinary milk-based drink into a real bar specialty.

Garnishes

Fresh fruit is to the cocktail what the "Flying Lady" is to a Rolls-Royce. Every well-stocked bar has lemons, limes, and oranges, primarily for making freshly squeezed juice. The emphasis here is on "fresh." Juices and fruit purees should always be made on the spot, otherwise they lose all their nutritional value. In the case of a freshly squeezed orange, the vitamins begin to degrade after just ten minutes.

Some of the citrus fruits should be organic, so that the peel can be used. Their highly aromatic, essential oils add a touch of class to many cocktails. The peel also makes a very good garnish: a long, thin strip wound over the top of the glass is eye catching. Some fruits can be used as fresh purees in drinks, so a blender is a great help. Peach puree (remember to take the skin off) is the distinguishing feature of a Bellini. And the pureed flesh of raspberries or passion fruit forms the flavorsome basis of champagne cocktails. In the profession, catering suppliers will deliver these products fresh and direct to your door.

Even if it is only to be used for decoration, a bartender should not skimp on fruit. Exotic fruit in particular can boost the visual appearance as well as the taste of a drink, as long as it is ripe. A piece of pineapple should not be sour but aromatic, just like a strawberry or banana slice. Customers will be more satisfied if the appetizing look of the garnish also delivers in terms of taste. A huge selection is available: seasonal berries, cape gooseberries, melons, mango, papaya... Slices of lemon or star fruit are more pleasing on the eye than the palate, but then of course no one expects to be able to eat them.

Fresh mint is essential for a Mojito, but it must be the right kind, without too much menthol to dull the taste buds. Suitable types are either Cuban mint (*Mentha nemorosa*) or spearmint.

Candied fruits are a simple answer to the issue of freshness. While lurid red Maraschino cherries with their cloying sweetness should remain a tribute to the 1960s, candied ginger, banana slices, and limes can prove quite successful in terms of experimentation.

Dry classics like a

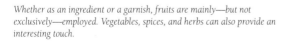

Whether as an ingredient or a garnish, fruits are mainly—but not exclusively—employed. Vegetables, spices, and herbs can also provide an interesting touch.

Vodka Gibson or Martini are best accompanied by pickled vegetables—olives (in brine, not stuffed with peppers), gherkins, or pearl onions.

Then there is cayenne pepper for cocktails with fresh cream, nutmeg for flips, cloves for mulled wine, and cinnamon sticks for punch. Salt, pepper, celery salt, and Tabasco and Worcestershire sauces liven up hangover drinks like the Bloody Mary.

If drinks have a classic garnish, like a piece of pineapple for a Piña Colada, think twice whether any change is necessary: a garnish that fits the contents of the drink makes sense, and that's that. You can give free rein to the imagination, on the other hand, when it comes to the loose interplay of a number of fruits, as in cobblers, fancies, and smoothies.

Basic

BUILDING IN A GLASS

Mixing a drink in the glass out of which it will be consumed must be the oldest way of making a cocktail. It is mainly used when the ingredients blend well together, that is when their gravitational weight is similar and any more intensive stirring or shaking would be superfluous. Usually these involve recipes that consist of two strong spirits or of a spirit and a juice. In terms of a glass, the best one to choose is a wide beaker. The ingredients are stirred together with ice in the glass and, depending on the recipe, they can be topped up with champagne or soda. Solid ingredients like sugar, lime, and mint are muddled in the empty glass, then topped with crushed ice and white rum in the case of a Mojito.

STIRRING IN A MIXING GLASS

Drinks to be served ice cold, preferably in an iced glass, or even with ice, should be stirred in a mixing glass big enough to hold enough ice cubes to chill the drink quickly, without melting too much. Liquids that need to be blended together only very lightly are also best in a mixing glass, especially if they are clear and would rapidly become cloudy in a shaker. Stirring should be done with a bar spoon for 20–30 seconds, using circular movements from the bottom of the glass upward, then strain through a Hawthorn sieve into the prepared glass. Ice from the mixing glass is discarded. For drinks served on ice, add fresh ice cubes or crushed ice to the glass.

techniques

SHAKING IN A SHAKER

Brandies, syrups, liqueurs, milk, and cream all have different gravitational weights and have to be mixed more energetically, so this is best done in a shaker. Carbonated drinks should, however, never be put in a shaker. Put the ingredients for at most three (two for a Boston shaker) drinks into the (glass) beaker with ice, seal on the metal part of the shaker, and then shake firmly for 10 seconds, or 20 for thicker juices or cream. It does not matter whether the shaking is horizontal or vertical: the most important thing is not to point it in the direction of the customer. Finally, the well-chilled drink can be strained through the bar sieve into the prepared glass.

MIXING WITH A BLENDER

Drinks with ice cream, egg yolk, or fresh fruit are best processed with an electric blender. Pour the measured ingredients onto ice cubes in the blender attachment. Again, in this case do not add carbonated liquids until after blending. Start slowly, increase the speed until the mixture is completely integrated, and then pour it into prepared glasses. When using an electric blender, especially for frozen drinks with a sorbet consistency, a little more sweetening is normally required.

Garnishing and serving

Each mixed drink is a minor work of art. The contents of the glass should be a tasty surprise and show true inspiration, for anyone ordering a drink in a bar does not expect a glass of just any old thing. What appears should catch the attention, not by cheap gimmicks but through the skilled composition of the individual parts. In doing so, less is usually more. As with ingredients, the purely decorative aspects of the fruit should concentrate on two to three features that enhance the basic expression of the drink.

The correct tools are needed to create the final touches. A plastic chopping board is required in the catering industry for cutting fresh fruit, though it is not ideal for the sharpness of the knives. Serrated knives are not as badly affected. Zesters and channel knives tear strips of different thicknesses from citrus fruit peel, which then twirl decoratively over or in the glass. Scoops are used for soft, fleshy fruit. Unless

Top: scooped melon balls

Left: fruit slices

hung on the edge of the glass as a decoration, most garnishes are lined up against the glass on wooden or plastic cocktail sticks. Empty sticks are also useful for chasing olives and pearl onions around the glass.

Garnishes are pretty add-ons, which above all must be in proportion. Too small is just as inappropriate as too big. Drinking straws are a must for drinks with crushed ice: they should be thick but not too long, and brightly colored. An excessive amount of fruit garnish is dubious enough, but the discomfiture level can easily increase when there are umbrellas, national flags, tinsel, or sparklers. What is justified cause for celebration on a child's birthday can sometimes ruin a visit to a bar.

Crustas, which are standard for some drinks, are purely a matter of taste as sugar and salt crystals or desiccated coconut on the rim of a glass can affect every sip. The crusta (sugared rim) is created by moistening the rim of the glass with a piece of citrus fruit, and then dipping the glass into the particular garnish. If blue curaçao or cassis is used for this, the edge becomes brightly colored.

Top: fine strips of lemon zest

Left: zest of citrus fruit

The mise-en-place

Mixing the perfect, tasty drink is a demanding job that entails quite a few maneuvers: all the more important, then, to prepare everything in advance, especially if several guests are to be served quickly. Virtually no one will use all of the things listed on the previous pages at the same time. Whether an amateur or a professional, each person can choose what to offer and make a note of everything required before shopping for the ingredients.

Once all the tools and ingredients are present, they have to be put into a meaningful order. The exact detail is up to the individual, but a few basic ground rules should be followed. Firstly, unnecessary journeys should be avoided, so everything should be within reach. Make sure shakers, measuring jugs, and chopping board are to hand. The electric blender and ingredients for garnishing should be on the work surface behind the bar.

The bottles can be problematic. They need to follow a logical order, grouped either by the type of drink or by the type of drink it goes into. Everyone will develop their own system here too, but the main thing is to be able to find all the important bottles without even looking.

Ice, fruit juices, and sodas should also be within reach of the workstation, ideally in a refrigerator under the work surface.

All that remains are the glasses. In many bars they hang on a glass rail above the bartender's head. In addition, a selection of cocktail glasses should be kept in the freezer compartment as shorts stay cold in these for longer.

Il Bar in the Bulgari Hotel, London is all set up and ready for the rush of guests.

82 | The mise-en-place

Mise-en-place in the Riva Bar in Düsseldorf's media harbor

Cocktails and drinks

Cocktails were around long before the first "American Bar" opened in Manhattan: ancient cultures are also known to have mixed alcoholic beverages. Cocktail culture itself, however, developed in the USA during the second half of the 19th century, made possible by America's melting pot of many immigrants, increasing prosperity, and the availability of products from the world over. By the 1920s cocktail bars had become an American institution that was soon imitated in Europe and the rest of the world.

"Drank a glass of cocktail—excellent for the head," was the cheerful declaration by an author writing in the Farmer's Cabinet on April 28, 1803. This is considered to be the first written mention of the name "cocktail." Professor Jerry Thomas published the first book of cocktails in 1862, his legendary Bartender's Guide or How to Mix Drinks. This makes mention of Sours, Slings, Flips, and other categories of mixed drinks. More and more Americans were taking to the colorful mixtures on offer in the bars. The Prohibition of 1920–33 banned the possession of alcohol in any form and so the owners of the speakeasies created mixtures as they saw fit in order to disguise it, but also to be able to make the best use of the hard to come by spirits. It was therefore the Prohibition that gave cocktail bars their first real boost.

Cocktails made more frequent appearances on the bar counters of Europe after World War II. It started with the bars in the grand hotels, but later every small town wanting to make a name for itself had to have a cocktail address. The often exaggerated glamor of the bars had become outdated by the end of the 1980s.

And hence the revival was all the more vibrant. The optimal ratio of tropical fruit juices, spirits, and syrups provides for almost unlimited options. This has long since been recognized by cocktail fans who often create imaginative combinations for themselves and their private audiences.

Left: the classic Rum Sour
Top: Fancy Vanilla Sky comes into the Whimsical category.

From highball to pick me up

Although cocktails and mixed drinks are (more or less) just pure pleasure and more especially fun, good barkeepers take a very serious and precise approach to them. Recipes are laid down with exact quantities and ingredients as the barkeepers love to see their guests' eyes light up when presented with a creative drink, something that they would like to see repeated as often as possible. A successful recipe therefore soon becomes a bar's best-kept secret.

The drinks are divided into groups, the members of which share specific properties. Hence one drink might be a colada because it is dominated by coconut and pineapple juice, another is a fizz because it is always topped with soda or lemonade. The group can also be determined by the spirit upon which the drinks are based.

Some of these groups themselves can be put together in categories based on a simple but useful criterion, namely quan-

tity. Drinks that incorporate only a little liquid and fit into a small glass such as a martini glass are called short drinks, sensibly enough. Long drinks are therefore those combinations containing fruit juices or soda that are best suited to filling a voluminous glass. The occasion also determines the category and so various groups can be classified as aperitifs or after-dinner drinks. Of course, some drinks fit into several groups, with new ones being added all the time. What was all the rage in a Caribbean bar five years ago has long since become history in a city club today. And so much the better, for every new mix makes it more interesting—even though, when you take a closer look, some of the new appearances are in fact the same as, or very similar to, that which went before.

It is therefore worth getting to know a couple of the groups, and this book classi-

Inspirational:
Negroni

Classic:
Pimm's No 1

Refreshing:
Tequila Smash

Fruity:
Starfish Cooler

Tropical:
French Col

fies drinks from classic to trendy, as well as from bitter pre-dinner drinks through to sweet combinations that are ordered after a meal or in the bar adjourned to after the meal. There are several recipes for each group, including typical examples and, more especially, suggestions for trying out these drinks categories and developing them further according to your own taste.

Cocktails and their "original recipes"

The first—and not the worst—mixed drinks were served more than 100 years ago. History-conscious barkeepers proudly offer drinks such as these which have been ennobled by their history. The basis for these recipes is almost always the earliest known mention, but that does not necessarily mean it was the original. What's more, in those days almost all spirits were produced with significantly fewer technical resources and contained considerably more pollutants than those produced today.

So anybody offering a classic based on the "original recipe" can never be entirely sure of being able to keep their promise.

Measures and abbreviations in the recipes
1 cl = 1 centiliter = 10 ml
1 bsp = 1 bar spoon = 0.5 cl
1 tbsp = 1 tablespoon = 1.5 cl
1 oz = 1 ounce = 3 cl
1 dash = 2–3 drops
Recipes usually have text and image placed one above the other.

Whimsical:
Passione

Invigorating:
Prairie Oyster

Salubrious:
Rainbow Warrior

Heated:
Jean Gabin

Virgin:
Hurricane Mocktail

Inspirational: bitter aperitifs

Talking of "bitter medicine" is hitting the nail right on the head when it comes to the raw ingredients for bitter aperitifs. Most of these herbs, roots, berries, and strips of peel were originally developed as medication. Ship's doctors used quinine to try to get sailors plagued with tropical infections back on their feet. In 1824 Dr. Johann Gottlieb Benjamin Siegert, the doctor with Simon Bolívar's army of freedom fighters in Venezuela, first tried out his bitter composition of 40 herbal extracts on soldiers with fever and stomach problems. The medication, which has become famous as a cocktail ingredient, was named after the town of Angostura where Siegert was stationed and not after the angostura bark, which is not included in the original recipe.

The sailors were quick to realize that they could make the bitter remedy much more pleasant to swallow by adding a little sugar and water and ensuring that they also had an alcoholic beverage to hand

Leonetto Cappiello was one of the most sought-after poster artists in the early 20th century.

at the same time. Most bitters were very high proof but, nevertheless, a drink such as Pink Gin (gin in a glass that had first been wiped out with a few drops of angostura) gained official status in the British navy. Today the dry taste of this bitter aperitif has become a classic before a meal and is a timeless appetite stimulant that periodically reinvents itself. For example, the German Jägermeister brand, with its romantic associations of woodsmen and elderly gentlemen, recently underwent a revival within the heavy metal scene. It was American stars from this set who discovered the herb liqueur as a party stimulant. The family-owned company from Wolfenbüttel in Germany that had originally developed the bitters recipe for medicinal purposes seized the opportunity and the biannual Jägermeister Music Tour promotes underground heavy metal bands, ensuring that "ice cold Jaeger" has since become an order often heard in American bars.

However, bitters appear much more frequently in mixed drinks. The intense bitter taste is ideal for combining with sweet flavors and sour citrus aromas. A simple Campari with orange juice is considered to be an accomplished aperitif or start to the evening. Many bitters have gone on to become legendary brand names since their invention in the 19th and early 20th centuries, thanks to successful marketing and poster campaigns. Fernet Branca, Suze or Becherovka, Campari, Cynar, and angostura are known in many countries around the world.

THAT CERTAIN AROMA

Whether it is a glass of champagne, a dry white wine, a malt, or a predinner cocktail, the aperitif has been a popular habit in Europe and beyond for a long time. Yet the outright winners are vermouth and other wine-based aperitifs, those Mediterranean invaders that vanquished preprandial tedium and ensured the smooth passage of food to the stomach. Who, then, can claim to have invented the aperitif? There is no shortage of contenders: the French and Italians each think it is their right, Spaniards view this with skepticism, and as far as the Greeks are concerned, it must surely have been them. Presumably they all did it simultaneously.

Inspirational: bitter aperitifs

Buñueloni

1 oz (3 cl) Punt e Mes
1 oz (3 cl) vermouth bianco
4 bsp (2 cl) gin
organic lemon and orange peel

Stir together in a small glass. Flavor with 1 piece each of lemon and orange peel.
Garnish with zest.

The Spanish director Luis Buñuel swore that he had never spent a day without this aperitif.

American Beauty

4 bsp (2 cl) dry vermouth
4 bsp (2 cl) vermouth rosso
3 tbsp (4 cl) brandy
1 dash grenadine
3 tbsp (4 cl) orange juice
tawny port

Stir in a measuring jug and pour into a chilled cocktail glass, topping with a little tawny port.

The drink will stay cold longer if you place the cocktail glass in a wide glass filled with crushed ice.

Negroni

1 oz (3 cl) vermouth rosso
1 oz (3 cl) Campari
1 oz (2–3 cl) gin
organic lemon peel
organic lemon or orange peel for garnishing

Stir together in an aperitif glass with ice cubes. Flavor with 1 piece of lemon peel, garnish with 1 strip of lemon or orange peel.

Variations: False Negroni with spumante instead of gin; Negroski with vodka instead of gin; Straight Up without ice, optionally with lemon juice and soda, top up with cola.

Columbo

1 oz (3 cl) Campari
4 bsp (2 cl) lime syrup
4 bsp (2 cl) lemon juice
3 tbsp (5 cl) orange juice

Shake together in a cold shaker, strain into a long glass over ice cubes, top up with tonic.

Where did this drink get its name? The inspector of the same name with the creased trench coat from the American TV series would perhaps be able to find out. He himself drank it very seldom.

Inspirational: champagne cocktails

Champagne Cocktail

1 sugar cube or 1 tsp granulated sugar
angostura
champagne

Place the sugar in a champagne glass and add a few drops of angostura. Top up with ice cold champagne.

There are some concoctions that must have been invented in heaven. A champagne cocktail is one of them.

Kir Royal

2 bsp (1 cl) crème de cassis
ice cold champagne

Pour crème de cassis into a champagne glass. Fill it up with ice cold champagne.

As mayor of Dijon, Felix Kir was a keen advocate of town twinning after World War I. In addition to mending social bridges, he managed to promote a local product beyond his region.

Bellini

white peaches
1–2 drops lemon juice
pêche mignon
sparkling wine

Remove the skin and pits from the peaches, puree them and add lemon juice and pêche mignon according to taste, place in a chilled champagne glass and stir. Top up with ice cold sparkling wine.

Champagne is also extraordinarily good in a Bellini.

French 75

4 bsp (2 cl) gin
2 bsp (1 cl) lemon juice
1 dash grenadine , 1 dash sugar syrup (optional)
champagne

Shake the first four ingredients together in a shaker with ice cubes and filter into a champagne glass; top up with champagne. Optional: decorate with a Cape gooseberry.

The name French 75 almost certainly refers to a French artillery cannon of World War I.

Inspirational: Manhattan

The Manhattan is always to be found at the top of the menu in a classic cocktail bar. A loner—dry, bitter, puritan, timeless. It is likely that the majority of guests who ordered it were men. Orders have now become more infrequent with the increasing popularity of tropical drinks. The Manhattan recently underwent a revival as one of the favorite drinks of Carrie Bradshaw (Sarah Jessica Parker), star of the television series Sex and the City, symbolizing her love of Manhattan life. Drinks were

Smoke in abundance:

Whisky. Whiskey. The word itself has a smoky ring to it. And it kindles associations. Images are evoked spontaneously: of distinctive pagoda towers, the landmark of distilleries in the Highlands; of Irish pubs in full swing; of the golden expanses of Kentucky and its racing horses. Anyone who appreciates whisk(e)y has a personal treasure trove of images and memories based on preference and travel experiences. For whisk(e)y—as the double way of spelling it suggests—is not a standard product. Quite the opposite, in fact.

What was originally drunk in the traditional whisk(e)y areas at first was a raw, high percent proof grain spirit, unless it was administered medicinally with added honey and herbs. Not until distillery owners and spirits merchants made a determined effort to tame its wild, fiery nature

Pagodas of Strathisla's drying kilns

Grains of green malt

already being prepared with the typical ingredients in the latter half of the 19th century in New York, where, on September 5, 1882, the Democrat newspaper stated that every barkeeper in town knew the recipe. Either way, drinks containing the Manhattan ingredients first appeared in New York City and consequently later acquired the name Manhattan.

A number of other whiskey combinations also go back to the early days of cocktails. With their whiskey character they are often very bitter, this often being offset by sweet components. The issue of the one and only true recipe soon leads to a clash with the purists. Today there are numerous dry (with more or less vermouth) and sweet versions. The Manhattan has also been a source of inspiration for many new drinks, including Rob Roy with Scotch, Cuban Manhattan with dark rum, Florida Manhattan with lime juice instead of angostura, Latin Manhattan with white rum and Maraschino, and Sake Manhattan with sake instead of vermouth.

whisky and whiskey

did it embark on its new course to global success. Achieving this was not just down to aging in casks, as blends (mixing lighter and stronger spirits together to make a harmonious whisk(e)y) also made a significant contribution. Although this is particularly typical of Scotland with its many malt and grain distilleries, it is equally applicable to Irish whiskey or American Bourbon, even if distilleries there only use separate spirits, albeit different ones, and the term "blend" is not one they like to hear.

Thus whiskies were created that appealed to a wide audience, and still do: they are best drunk on the rocks, in long drinks, or in cocktails.

Drying kilns use heat and smoke

Distillation in pot stills

Inspirational: Manhattan

Manhattan

3 tbsp (5 cl) Canadian whisky
1 oz (2.5 cl) vermouth rosso
1–2 drops angostura
1 cocktail cherry for garnishing

Stir the first two ingredients together and add the angostura in a mixing glass with lots of ice cubes. Pour into a chilled cocktail glass and stir. Garnish with 1 cocktail cherry.

This is the favorite drink of the International Bartenders Association (IBA).

Whiskey Sangaree

2 bsp (1 cl) granulated sugar
2 oz (6 cl) rye or Bourbon
soda
1 tbsp (1.5 cl) port
ground nutmeg

Dissolve the sugar in a tumbler of water, add the rye or Bourbon and ice cubes. Stir and top up with soda, float port on top, and sprinkle with a little ground nutmeg.

New Orleans Sazerac

1 bsp granulated sugar
angostura
2 oz (6 cl) Bourbon
2 bsp (1 cl) pastis
organic lemon peel

Place the sugar in a tumbler, add a couple of dashes of angostura and ice cubes. Pour in Bourbon and pastis, add lemon peel, stir, and top up with a shot of ice cold water.

Sazeracs are among the oldest of cocktails, first served in 1859 at the opening of the Sazerac Coffee House in New Orleans.

Old Fashioned

1 bsp granulated sugar
a few drops of angostura
3 organic lemon wedges
3 organic orange slices
2 oz (6 cl) Bourbon
1 cocktail cherry for garnishing

Place the first four ingredients in a large tumbler ("Old Fashioned Glass") and press down with a plunger. Add some Bourbon, stir, add ice cubes, top up with water, and garnish with a cocktail cherry.

Classic: sours

A sour can be seen as the ancestor of many of today's well-known mixed drinks. Spirits, sugar, something sour—that's it. Famous drinks such as the Margarita, White Lady, Daiquiri, and Sidecar are basically sours and, apart from the fact that ice cubes were added later to give them a frosty touch, the ingredients remain the same today.

The sweet component can be provided by a syrup such as grenadine or by a liqueur such as triple sec. In terms of the "hard tack," there is hardly any high-proof spirit that is not suited to a

Times of plenty

It is no secret that the art of whiskey distilling in the United States can be traced back to Scottish and Irish immigrants. After the 1745 Jacobite Rebellion in Scotland, the notorious Highland Clearances took place, as a result of which thousands of peasant farmers were driven from their leaseholdings and forced to emigrate. Mass emigration also took place in Ireland. The destination of choice for those emigrating, many of whom were skilled in the art of distillation, was the east coast of North America. Though barley was not a thriving crop there, rye made up for it.

So the first American whiskey was almost certainly a rye. The earliest recorded dis-

Life in Lynchburg has always been rural.

Barrels on their way to the Jack Daniel's Distillery

sour. The list of recipes is therefore correspondingly long. About 2 oz (6 cl) of the basis spirit is mixed with 1 oz (3 cl) of the sweet component and 1 tbsp (1.5 cl) of lemon or lime juice. The proportions vary with every drink. Gin has a different effect compared to rum, an American whiskey behaves differently from Scotch. The proportions are therefore best adjusted by tasting the concoction after mixing.

Despite the endless variations, some sours have managed to achieve lasting fame. A prime example is the sour made from pisco which goes especially well with fresh lemon juice and a few drops of bitters. The softness of brandy is used in a Brandy Daisy, for example. In tropical regions it is often sweetened with curaçao. The Whiskey Sour is a traditional southern states drink in the USA.

and new beginnings

tillery, Michter's, was founded in Schaefferstown in 1753 and continued to operate until 1988.

The immigrants traveled further west across the Allegheny mountains, where they were promised land on condition that they raise crops on it. Bourbon County (now part of Virginia and Kentucky) was founded there in 1785, and was named for the French royal house that had supported America's fight for independence. Corn grew in abundance on the vast plains, presenting a downright invitation to distill it. As whiskey sold well, many farmers made it their main source of income. They labeled their casks "Old Bourbon" and shipped them over the Ohio and Mississippi rivers to New Orleans. There folk enjoyed the taste of the unusual whiskey with its sweet, full flavor, and soon it became known as "Bourbon."

The rise in production saw a growth not only in the social problems caused by alcohol abuse, but also in the abstinence movement. By 1855 12 states were "dry" and in 1920 Prohibition came into force across the whole country.

Only a few producers had the courage to start over in 1933, and Jim Beam was the first. As if he had just been waiting at the age of 70 to be able to carry on the family tradition, he set up the new distillery in Clermont in 1934. Heaven Hill in Bardstown opened the following year. In the decades that followed a few companies managed to establish a name for themselves internationally. Alongside Jim Beam there were Wild Turkey, Four Roses, and Jack Daniel's. It took until 1964, however, for the US Congress to recognize ourbon as a "distinctive product of the United States," defining and protecting it by law.

In 1866 Jack Daniel founded his distillery.

Classic: sours

Gin Sour

3 tbsp (4 cl) gin
4 bsp (2 cl) lemon juice
1 tbsp (1.5 cl) sugar syrup
1 cocktail cherry for garnishing

Shake together in a shaker and filter into a small goblet with ice cubes. Garnish with a cocktail cherry.

Whiskey Sour

3 tbsp (4 cl) Bourbon
4 bsp (2 cl) lemon juice
1 tbsp (1.5 cl) sugar syrup
2 cocktail cherries for garnishing

Shake in a shaker and filter into a small goblet with ice cubes. Garnish with 2 cocktail cherries.

Rum Sour

3 tbsp (4 cl) dark rum
4 bsp (2 cl) lemon juice
4 bsp (2 cl) curaçao
1 cocktail cherry for garnishing

Shake in a shaker and filter into a small goblet with ice cubes. Garnish with a cocktail cherry.

Pisco Sour

3 tbsp (4 cl) pisco
4 bsp (2 cl) lemon juice
1–2 drops angostura according to taste
1 tbsp (1.5 cl) sugar syrup
1 cocktail cherry for garnishing

Shake together in a shaker and filter into a small goblet with ice cubes. Garnish with 1 cocktail cherry.

Classic: martinis and gin drinks

The martini appeared in a cocktail book as early as 1862 but it was during the American Prohibition that it really gained in popularity. During this crisis era whiskey, which needs to be matured for a number of years, became a lot more difficult to acquire than gin—which could be produced using primitive "bathtub" equipment. The gin/vodka concoction has been declared the favorite drink of American movie stars, as well as writers and politicians, time and again. The list extends

Gin

Gin owes its taste not to the basic grain. Maturation in barrels has little to do with it either. Gin takes its life from spices, and in particular juniper. Nevertheless, gins differ widely depending on the recipe used.

Old Tom is a gin in the slightly sweet style of the 18th century. Gin historians like to refer to it as the missing link between original Dutch genever and the English style.

Somewhat drier but solid is Plymouth Gin, which likes to portray itself as mellowest of the world's gins. Aromatic herbs and fewer bitter flavors with soft water to round off distinguish the Plymouth style. Blow its own trumpet as it might, the spirit from the old naval port is actually very full

Above: juniper; below: licorice　　　*Above: coriander; below: violet root*

from Franklin D. Roosevelt to Truman Capote and from Cary Grant to Robert Oppenheimer.

The martini has become so synonymous with the cocktail that the conical stemware cocktail glass is often simply referred to as a martini glass. The society critic Henry Louis Mencken once called the martini "the only American invention, the perfection of which is comparable to a sonnet."

The British James Bond also had a significant input to the topic of martinis, always insisting that his martini be "shaken, not stirred." In the opinion of professional barkeepers that is precisely the wrong way round. In principle two clear spirits are always stirred. Shaking dilutes the drink and makes it cloudy.

The correct ratio of vermouth to gin is the subject of endless debate, with the vermouth component having become smaller and smaller. Winston Churchill liked his gin to be ice cold and while drinking it he did no more than cast a glance at the bottle of vermouth.

secrets

bodied, roundly sweet, without any hint of sharpness.

Unsweetened but often aromatic gins are characteristic of the British production and bear the label "London dry." As well as junipers, there dominate here often lemon and orange zest, together with aniseed, cinnamon, coriander, violet root, licorice, and angelica. Cassia bark and pepper varieties also feature. No matter how the aromatic herbs may differ in intensity, the spirit always remains free of sugary sweetness. London dry gins are now the most widespread.

Above: Malagueta pepper; below: cassia bark   *Above: angelica; below: lemon zest*

Classic: martinis and gin drinks

Alexander

....

3 tbsp (4 cl) cream
1 oz (3 cl) gin
4 bsp (2 cl) crème de cacao

Thoroughly shake in a shaker, filter into a cocktail glass
and sprinkle with a little nutmeg.

AROMA DOWN TO A FINE ART

By contrast with many other alcohol producers, gin producers generally avoid distilling their base spirit themselves, preferring to be supplied with neutral 96% by volume alcohol. However, all brand producers stress their preference for grain as being a finer, more aromatic base and refuse alcohol from other raw ingredients, in particular molasses.

Therefore the gin distilleries concentrate from the start on the fine art of aromatization. Each brand has its own recipe in which various natural aromatic substances appear in varying combinations. More often than not house methods are maintained—usually out of tradition.

In England, the stronghold of gin distillation, this second cycle takes place in copper pot stills. Normally pure alcohol and water are placed in the pot still. Its quality will have an effect on the final product that is not to be underestimated. Then the aromatic mixture is poured straight into the liquid and distilled. Other distilleries have moved towards suspending their aromatic substances in a heat-resistant net or basket in the still—there are models designed with an appropriate device—so that the rising alcohol vapor is drawn through them and takes on the volatile aromatic substances. Some traditional producers are proud of the fact that the mixture of various plants and plant parts is macerated for some time in alcohol first, so that the aromatic molecules are more thoroughly absorbed.

Martini Cocktail

5 tbsp (8 cl) gin
4 bsp (2 cl) dry vermouth
stuffed olives for garnishing

Stir together in a mixing glass with ice cubes until the glass becomes frosted. Alternatively, place the cocktail glass in the refrigerator beforehand. Garnish with stuffed olives.

Eccentrics allow themselves olives filled with almonds.

Parisienne

4 bsp (2 cl) Noilly Prat
4 bsp (2 cl) gin
1–2 drops crème de cassis, 1 olive for garnishing

Stir together with ice and filter into a cocktail glass. Garnish with an olive.

For a more sophisticated version, pour the crème de cassis into the cocktail glass first, then add the clear ingredients. Guests are then able to mix the two layers themselves using a cocktail stick.

Classic: multitalents

Earthquake

1 part absinthe
1 part brandy

Combine in a cold mixing glass. Serve in a large goblet with ice cubes.

The drink stands up to its name. It is recommended that you temper it with a little water and sugar.

Strawberry Margarita

3 tbsp (5 cl) tequila
3 tbsp (5 cl) triple sec
1 oz (2.5 cl) lime juice
2 oz (50 g) strawberries, fresh or deep frozen
1 strawberry for garnishing

Puree the ingredients with ice in a blender. Depending on the ripeness of the fruit, sweeten with confectioners' sugar or strawberry syrup. Pour into a cocktail glass. Garnish with 1 strawberry on the rim.

Bahía

1 oz (3 cl) white rum
3 tbsp (4 cl) pineapple juice
2 bsp (1 cl) coconut syrup
1 oz (3 cl) coconut cream
1 oz (3 cl) sweetened cream
pineapple and cocktail cherries for garnishing

Thoroughly shake in a shaker. Filter into a tumbler of crushed ice, and garnish with a piece of pineapple and cocktail cherries.

Thug Passion

2 oz (6 cl) Alizé
2 oz (6 cl) champagne

Stir Alizé in a cold mixing glass, filter into a narrow champagne flute, and top up with champagne.

The concoction was the rapper 2Pac's favorite drink and he even dedicated one of his songs to it. The singer himself used Roederer Cristal for the sparkle and always had some available at home. If you find its retail price of € 250 for one bottle to be a bit much, you can of course use a different sparkling wine.

Classic: vodka

The emergence of mixed drinks in the USA and England toward the middle of the 19th century brought with it numerous recipes using gin, rum, and whiskey. Bitters and vermouth, imported from Italy and France, were the trendy drinks of the time and included rare specialties among them. Vodka remained an outsider at first, the potato and grain liquor only asserting itself in the 20th century but then all the more dominantly. Its neutral taste meant it was the obvious choice for any kind of fruit juice, as well as for bitters, liqueur, and lemonade. Vodka, which is especially pure and mild due to activated carbon filtering, is a spirit that suits almost any ingredient used in a bar and is to be found in the proximity of any drink dominated by fruit and fruit juices.

Its rise was so rapid that, following World War II, it soon overtook all other spirits on the American market. The United States remain the world's largest vodka consumers today. Even during the cold war it made no difference that vodka was popular in communist Russia. In order to make it clear that it was a US product—made from American grain—the later market leader Smirnov promptly changed its name to Smirnoff and used the advertising slogan: "Smirnoff White Whiskey. No Taste. No Smell."

Despite its late start, vodka still managed to have a number of classics make it on to bar menus around the world, often stealing ground from its older competitors in the process. Drinks that were originally made with gin have since become popular with vodka as well.

Russian Standard Vodka (opposite) is distilled in St. Petersburg from top quality wheat from the Russian Steppes.

Absolut quality

Where once the roles were very clearly defined, over recent decades the composition of grain spirits has started to change. The initiative here came from vodka—now the world's most popular spirit—and, first and foremost, Swedish Absolut. Even before it made its appearance on the American market toward the end of the 1970s some brands had managed to carve out market shares for themselves (the prevalent belief being that vodka in cocktails really only affected the alcohol content), but Absolut became the first real star in the premium vodka segment. The fact that it became chic to drink a particular brand was not least due to a brilliant marketing strategy and a new bottle design.

In the early 1990s international vodka brands such as Moskovskaya and Stolichnaya added prestige variants to their normal products. For the past ten years or so, vodkas have been available that can only be described as ultra-premium. Starting from the assumption that nothing is as luxurious as the purest of the pure, experts have developed sophisticated concepts for making their distillates ever more mellow, ever clearer, and ever more elegant.

Although, according to experts, it has not been possible to improve on the manufacturing methods for a number of years, the quality of the product has been enhanced within the limits of imagination and creativity.

Only water from a glacier or from a well 330 feet (100 m) deep will do to dilute the six or seven times distilled noble spirit to drinking strength. Activated carbon must be used for filtration at precisely 32 °F (0 °C) or, even better, silver or diamonds. Bottling must be at least into crystal.

Classic: vodka

Sea Breeze

2 oz (6 cl) vodka
3 tbsp (4 cl) cranberry juice
2 oz (6 cl) grapefruit juice
1 Cape gooseberry
1 slice of star fruit
1 shot cranberry juice

Shake the vodka, cranberry juice, and grapefruit juice together on ice. Filter into a tall glass filled with ice, garnish with the fruit, and add the cranberry juice.

Pimm's No 19

4 bsp (2 cl) vodka
4 bsp (2 cl) Pimm's
4 bsp (2 cl) Galliano
ginger ale
cucumber for garnishing

Pour the vodka, Pimm's, and Galliano into a tumbler with ice cubes, stir and top up with ginger ale. Garnish with cucumber.

WHITE RUSSIAN

The White Russian owes its name solely to the vodka element. Nevertheless, it is a very popular drink in the USA and is inextricably linked with pop culture. For example, the character The Dude played by Jeff Bridges "floats" through the cult movie The Big Lebowski with one. The British band Marillion dedicated a song to the drink in 1987. White Russian drinkers are experimenters and risk takers.

Here are just a few of the variations in existence:
COLORADO BULLDOG with vanilla vodka and cola
WHITE TRASH with whiskey instead of vodka
GAY RUSSIAN with cherry brandy instead of Kahlúa
KGB with high proof vodka
ANNA KOURNIKOVA with skimmed milk
BLONDE RUSSIAN with Irish Cream instead of cream
COCAINE LADY with peppermint liqueur and milk
COLIN POWELL with cocoa
VAN HOWELL SPECIAL with amaretto and rum

Gibson Vodka

3 tbsp (5 cl) vodka
1 dash dry vermouth
pearl onions

Stir the vodka and vermouth in a mixing glass with plenty of ice. Filter into a chilled cocktail glass. Pearl onions in the glass are the hallmark of this drink.

White Russian

3 tbsp (4 cl) vodka
1 oz (2.5 cl) Kahlúa or another coffee liqueur
lightly whipped cream
coffee or cocoa for garnishing (optional)

Stir the vodka and Kahlúa well in a mixing glass with ice cubes. Filter into a cocktail glass and add cream. Garnish with a little coffee or cocoa according to taste.

Classic: shooters and short drinks

Be it a conservative club or a wild techno location, even though the drinks served might be different, a shooter is drunk at every bar sooner or later. The quick kick is simply a must. Shooters are often ordered by groups and ensure a party atmosphere in next to no time. The names of the shooters are a graphic illustration of both the objective and the effect: Aftershock, Kamikaze, Gorilla Fart, Four Horsemen. The orders are as diverse as the guests, and some of them are very witty.

The tequila

The *fábricas* swear by tequila consisting of 100% blue agave, fermented with natural yeast existing in the vats that have been used over the years, from which however they have often cultivated their own strains. Depending on the variety of yeast and temperature, fermentation can last from 5 to 12 days and has a significant impact on the aromas of the *mosto* or must and the subsequent tequila. Soil, altitude, climate, location, and also the degree of maturity and time of harvesting—as well as the cooking method—are other factors affecting the character of the aroma.

As soon as the agave must is fully fermented, it is filtered and pumped into the pot still. Distillation is in two cycles: first the *ordinario*, which is between 20 and 30% alcohol by vol., condenses. It is distilled the second time into tequila. As

Agaves, the secret ingredient of Sierra Tequila

The jimador removes the agave leaves.

A shooter and a beer to wash it down is a popular order going by the name of Boilermaker or Car Bomb. A lot depends on the spirits used: the explosive mixture can become an Irish Car Bomb if there is Irish Whiskey in the liqueur glass. The different varieties possible have had the real experimenters drinking two at a time. A tradition observed in many countries is the Submarine (photo p. 114) that has a liqueur placed in a large filled beer mug. True fans empty the mug in one go and then wait to see what happens. Different spirits are used depending on the locality. Jägermeister is popular, while vodka is more of a classic, allegedly from Poland. Modern versions have the shooter immersed into Red Bull (also known as Jägerbomb.) The heaviest weapon, the Nuclear Submarine, goes to anyone who can down the quantities in the reverse ratio with a small beer immersed in a large liqueur.

story

with all fractional distillation processes, the distiller separates off the heads and tails (*cabeza* and *cola*), and only collects the heart (*corazon*). Traditionally tequila is distilled with an alcohol content of 55% by vol.—i.e. the heart is rather great, which gives the distillate more bite and aroma—but also means that it contains more fusel oil. Modern producers distill at a higher degree, often as much as three times as high, in order to achieve greater mellowness (and more neutrality) and finally to reduce the distillate to a drinkable strength. The American market in particular prefers more mellow qualities. On average 15 lb (7 kg) of agave hearts are required for 2 pints (1 liter) of tequila.

Agave hearts are baked in ovens.

Sierra Tequila Reposado matures in oak barrels.

Classic: shooters and short drinks

Tequila Slammer

1 part tequila
1 part tonic or lemonade (Seven Up, ginger ale)

Combine the tequila and tonic or lemonade (Seven Up, ginger ale), cover with a beer mat and slam down onto the table.

Lemon Drop

Lemon juice for rim
Sugar
1 tbsp (1.5 cl) lemon vodka
1 tbsp (1.5 cl) lemon juice

Dip the rim of a liqueur glass in lemon juice first and then in sugar. Fill the glass with the lemon vodka and lemon juice. As in many drinks, the alcohol is tamed by the sweetness or the fruity acid.

Gold Rush

1 tbsp (1.5 cl) dark tequila
1 tbsp (1.5 cl) Danziger Goldwasser

Combine the ingredients to produce an upmarket shooter with a touch of glamour.

Still a shooter, but one with style.

◄ Submarine

Classic: legends

Pimm's No 1

3 tbsp (5 cl) Pimm's
Seven Up
cucumber for garnishing

Fill a large tumbler with crushed ice. Add the Pimm's, top up with Seven Up, and garnish with cucumber.

Ritz

4 bsp (2 cl) orange juice
4 bsp (2 cl) cognac
1 tbsp (1.5 cl) Cointreau
champagne
grape and orange for garnishing

Shake the orange juice, cognac, and Cointreau in a shaker, filter into a champagne glass, and top up with champagne. Garnish with a slice of grape and a slice of orange.

Sidecar

3 tbsp (4 cl) cognac
4 bsp (2 cl) Cointreau
4 bsp (2 cl) lemon juice
orange and lemon wedges for garnishing

Shake the cognac, Cointreau, and lemon juice well in a
shaker and filter into a small goblet with ice cubes.
Garnish with orange and lemon wedges.

Tipperary

3 tbsp (4.5 cl) Irish whiskey
1 oz (3 cl) vermouth bianco
1 tbsp (1.5 cl) Chartreuse (green)
1 cocktail cherry for garnishing

Combine the Irish whiskey, vermouth bianco, and green
Chartreuse over ice cubes and filter into a cocktail glass.
Garnish with the cocktail cherry.

Refreshing: classic long drinks

A long drink has two obvious advantages that significantly reduce the risk of drinking too much alcohol at the bar too early in the evening. It contains less alcohol in relation to many short drinks and comprises a relatively large quantity of water or juice. Understandably, highballs soon became one of the most ordered drinks. Creating a highball itself is child's play as the simplest combinations are based on one part spirits with three to five parts lemonade or juice. It was this simple rec-

Endless

In the world of spirits liqueurs are something extra special. Their colors alone give an immediate hint of what is to come, confirmed by the first sip. From curative herbal elixirs to enticing creations made from exotic fruits.

It is no surprise that liqueurs are so popular, for in the current profusion of choice there will be one to suit everybody. The palette ranges from rich, dry herbal cordials to fresh, fruity specialties and velvety, sweet temptations made with cream and honey. It is hard to imagine there were times when most folk had to do without these indulgences. Sugar was expensive and it took so much of it to produce liqueurs that they became delicacies beyond the reach of the average citizen (this also explains

Raw materials for liqueur production at De Kuyper

The maceration process begins in large tanks.

ipe that brought rapid fame to the Cuba Libre, the Screwdriver, and the like.

A Time Magazine reporter made an interesting observation in the bar of the New York Park Hotel on October 24, 1949. He saw Balkan refugees, American engineers, and Turkish secret service agents interacting peacefully with one another over a long drink, discreetly stirring the orange juice and vodka mixture with a screwdriver. In the 1970s the Screwdriver was considered the healthiest of alcoholic drinks due to its high Vitamin C content.

The officers of the British East India Company praised the gin and tonic combination for its medicinal effects for their staff. Long drinks have continued their rise to fame in almost all inhabited areas, including those that have still to be explored—such as outer space in The Hitchhiker's Guide to the Galaxy, where gin and tonic puts in an infinite range of appearances. The classics in this category include the following four long drinks on the next two pages.

possibilities

why many of the old recipes use the natural sweetness of honey). In the good old days those without means would only get the chance to sip the mysterious concoctions if they were sick, for monks skilled in the art of healing would mix liqueurs as medicine.

At the beginning of the 19th century sugar from the colonies and from domestic fields became cheaper, so liqueurs have long since changed from status symbols to public property. There is a liqueur for every occasion: the elegant bitter liqueur as an aperitif, the robust herbal cordial as a digestif, the sweet fruit creme liqueur with coffee, and the seductive cream-based liqueur in any of the intervening moments...

By-product: berries preserved in alcohol

Precious liquids at liqueur specialist De Kuyper

Refreshing: classic long drinks

Singapore Sling

3 tbsp (4 cl) gin
1 tbsp (1.5 cl) cherry liqueur
2 bsp (1 cl) Bénédictine
4 bsp (2 cl) lime juice
1 tbsp (1.5 cl) sugar syrup
soda, cocktail cherries

Stir the first five ingredients together in a cold mixing glass. Filter into a tall glass with crushed ice, top up with soda, and garnish with cocktail cherries.

Since 1915 anyone who has not enjoyed a Singapore Sling at the Long Bar in the Raffles Hotel is regarded as not having been to Singapore.

Long Island Ice Tea

4 bsp (2 cl) white rum
4 bsp (2 cl) vodka
4 bsp (2 cl) tequila
4 bsp (2 cl) gin
4 bsp (2 cl) triple sec
2 drops lime juice
cola
1 slice lemon

Shake the first six ingredients in a shaker. Filter into a tall glass with plenty of ice and top up with cola. The ingredients can vary. A slice of lemon on the rim alludes to tea.

Prince of Wales

1 sugar cube (or 1 bsp sugar)
1 dash angostura
1 oz (2.5 cl) cognac
2 bsp (1 cl) Bénédictine
2 orange quarters, 1 cocktail cherry
champagne or sparkling wine

Soak the sugar cube in a dash of angostura in a large glass. Add the cognac and Bénédictine, top up with crushed ice, then add the orange quarters and cocktail cherry, finishing with champagne or sparkling wine.

The Prince of Wales is one of the few examples of a mixed drink with the perfect balance between bitter, sweet, and sour that retains the noble taste of its high-quality ingredients.

Hurricane

4 bsp (2 cl) white rum
1 oz (3 cl) dark rum
2 bsp (1 cl) pineapple juice
2 bsp (1 cl) lemon juice
2 oz (6 cl) passion fruit juice
2 bsp (1 cl) sugarcane syrup
citrus peel for garnishing

Thoroughly shake all of the ingredients in a shaker. Filter into a hurricane glass with crushed ice, and garnish with citrus peel.

The sailors in the French quarter of New Orleans knew how to cope with tropical cyclones. The regulars took the Hurricane so much to heart that today it is even available in instant powder form.

Refreshing: highballs

Horse's Neck

3 tbsp (4 cl) brandy
7 tbsp (11 cl) ginger ale
1 dash angostura
lemon peel for garnishing (optional)

Pour the brandy into an Old Fashioned glass with ice cubes, stir, and top up with ginger ale, adding a dash of angostura according to taste. Garnish with lemon peel if liked.

A drink with a name as unusual as its history, it first appeared in the 1890s as a soft drink. The first brandy versions had appeared by 1910, as had those with Bourbon and rye, ultimately displacing the alcohol-free versions.

Harvey Wallbanger

3 tbsp (5 cl) vodka
8 tbsp (12 cl) orange juice, 1 shot Galliano

Pour the vodka and orange juice into a tall glass with ice and stir. Add a shot of Galliano, stirring briefly.

According to legend, Harvey was a Californian surfer. Following a lost competition he consoled himself in Duke's Blackwatch Bar in Hollywood with this sophisticated Screwdriver. Of course he did not stick to one, and Harvey banged into the walls on his way out. The rest is bar history. Whenever elections are held in the United States a significant proportion of spoiled votes are for a certain Harvey Wallbanger.

Cuba Libre

3 tbsp (5 cl) white rum
3 oz (10 cl) cola
1 dash lime juice
lime slices

Pour the white rum and cola into a tall glass with ice. Stir and add a dash of lime juice. Add some lime slices to the glass and the most famous drink in the world is ready.

The name does not derive from the socialist revolution of 1959, however. Legend has it that the drink was invented by soldiers in a bar in Havana drinking to the "liberation" of Cuba during the Spanish–American wars of the 1900s. Since both at that time and later original Coca-Cola was not available in Cuba, lemonade would have been an original component.

Sex on the Beach

3 tbsp (4 cl) vodka
4 bsp (2 cl) Pêche Mignon, 3 tbsp (4 cl) orange juice
3 tbsp (4 cl) cranberry juice
berries and orange slice for garnishing

Stir the vodka, Pêche Mignon, and orange juice together in a Highball glass with ice. Top up with the cranberry juice and garnish with the fruit.

No need to ask which came first, the drink or the name. However, whether it is named after the famous scene in the movie *From Here to Eternity* (USA 1953), after the summer hit by the pop group T-Spoon, or after a leisure activity that is illegal in many countries is open to debate.

Refreshing: fizzes and Collinses

A fizz has an extra portion of soda compared to a sour and is often served in bars with lemon or lime juice. It is the somewhat spiced-up version of the sour. The term "fizz" first appeared at the end of the 19th century when carbonated water became more readily available. The fizzing element makes the drink livelier and softer. The ingredients are easily available and it is merely a question of the mix ratio. A fizz is considered to be a refreshing drink during the day as well as later. Like sours, the fizzes' appeal derives from the clarity of their ingredients. There is one prominent spirit instead of an endless row of homogeneous forms of alcohol, which is then combined with the classic ingredients of sugar, citrus fruit, and water. There is no hiding anything behind a dominant ingredient here. A fizz made from cheap gin will taste cheap.

The Gin Fizz is the most well-known member of the family. This may be due to the fact that it goes exceptionally well with the lemon and soda combination, as is proved by the many variations such as the Silver Fizz with egg white, the Golden Fizz with egg yolk, and the Diamond Fizz with sparkling wine instead of soda.

Collinses (also known as cobblers) are close relatives of the fizzes. Their ingredients are not shaken but are stirred in the glass and then usually topped up with a little more soda, making them ideally suited to hot summer afternoons.

Daisies and crustas are XXXL-size drinks. They need big glasses with lots of ice, lots of liquid, and lots of alcohol. These refreshments should not be underestimated, therefore. Traditionally, they are made with gin or brandy plus lemon juice and sugar. The crusta has a sugared rim as an additional feature.

FAMILY SAGA IN BRIEF

Jack Collins	with Calvados
Tom Collins	with gin
Sandy / Jock Collins	with Scotch
John Collins	with rye whiskey
Captain Collins	with Canadian whisky
Mike Collins	named after the Irish revolutionary leader and later Finance Minister, Michael Collins
Colonel Collins	with Bourbon
Pedro Collins	with white rum
Ron Collins	with dark rum
Pisco Collins	with pisco
José Collins	with tequila
Comrade Collins	with vodka
Brandy Collins	with brandy
Pierre Collins	with cognac
Phil Collins	with tequila, Irish whiskey, vodka, rum, and beer.

Calvados

APPLE SCHOOLS AND APPLE CONCERTS

The Normans have known how to treat apples and pears for centuries and the range of varieties grown here is legendary. However, you need to be wary of simply biting into many of these fruit: they develop their unique charm only when they are ready for drinking, as cider and poiré, bitter or sweet, gently sparkling or bubbling vigorously, and ultimately reduced to their very essence as Calvados. Once you know that some kinds of Calvados are a combination of two, three, even four dozen different apple varieties—with Domfrontais even containing pears—then its wonderfully diverse bouquet and rounded flavor is no longer quite such a mystery.

Long before Calvados was considered to be worthy of bearing the name of its home region, this apple brandy was helping the rural population to bear the cold and wet of Normandy.

Its real rise to fame, however, like that of cider too, began in the 1980s when the interest in authentic products grew worldwide. These days, its distinctly fruity aromas make Calvados essential to the better class of bar.

Apples are machine-harvested and pressed in a rack and cloth press.

Mobile alembics are still used today, and oak plays a key role in maturation.

Refreshing: fizzes and Collinses

Gin Fizz

3 tbsp (5 cl) gin
1 oz (3 cl) lemon juice
4 bsp (2 cl) sugar syrup
soda

Shake the gin, lemon juice, and sugar syrup in a shaker
with ice. Filter into a tall glass half filled with crushed ice
and top up with soda.

Ramos Gin Fizz

3 tbsp (4 cl) gin
1 tbsp (1.5 cl) sugar syrup
1 egg white
4 bsp (2 cl) cream
1 dash orange-flower water
soda

Thoroughly shake the first five ingredients in a shaker.
Filter into a tall glass with ice cubes and top up with
soda.

Jack Collins

3 tbsp (4 cl) Calvados
4 bsp (2 cl) lemon juice
4 bsp (2 cl) sugar syrup
soda
lemon peel for garnishing
1 cocktail cherry for garnishing (optional)

Stir the Calvados, lemon juice, and sugar syrup in a tall glass with ice cubes and top up with soda. Garnish with a strip of lemon peel and a cocktail cherry according to taste.

Tom Collins

3 tbsp (4 cl) gin
4 bsp (2 cl) lemon juice
1 tbsp (1.5 cl) sugar syrup
soda
lemon peel for garnishing
1 cocktail cherry for garnishing (optional)

Stir the gin, lemon juice, and sugar syrup in a tall glass with ice cubes and top up with soda. Garnish with a strip of lemon peel and a cocktail cherry according to taste.

Refreshing: fizzes

Morning Glory Fizz

3 tbsp (5 cl) Scotch
1 oz (2.5 cl) lemon juice
4 bsp (2 cl) sugar syrup
1 egg white
1 shot pastis
soda
lemon and berries for garnishing

Thoroughly shake the first five ingredients in a shaker with ice. Filter into a tall glass with ice cubes and top up with soda. Garnish with lemon and/or berries.

Sloe Gin Fizz

3 tbsp (4 cl) sloe gin
4 bsp (2 cl) lemon juice
1 tbsp (1.5 cl) sugar syrup
soda
lemon and/or berries for garnishing

Thoroughly shake the sloe gin, lemon juice, and sugar syrup in a shaker. Filter into a tumbler with ice cubes and top up with soda. Garnish with lemon and/or berries. Sloe gin is a gin liqueur made with sloes.

Green Fizz

3 tbsp (4 cl) gin
1 shot crème de menthe
4 bsp (2 cl) lemon juice
4 bsp (2 cl) sugar syrup
soda

Shake the first four ingredients in a shaker with ice. Filter
into a tumbler with ice cubes and top up with soda.
The mint liqueur makes the drink all the more refreshing.

Chicago Fizz

1 oz (3 cl) white rum
1 oz (3 cl) port
4 bsp (2 cl) lemon juice
2 bsp (1 cl) sugar syrup
soda
lemon slices and berries for garnishing

Shake the first four ingredients in a shaker with ice. Filter
into a tall glass with ice cubes and top up with soda.
Garnish with lemon slices and berries.

Refreshing: daisies and crustas

Gin Daisy

2 oz (6 cl) gin
4 bsp (2 cl) lemon juice
4 bsp (2 cl) grenadine
soda
preserved morello cherries for garnishing

Shake the gin, lemon juice, and grenadine in a shaker
and filter into a large glass of crushed ice. Top up with
soda and garnish with cherries.

Applejack Daisy

3 tbsp (4.5 cl) Calvados
1 oz (3 cl) brandy
3 tbsp (4.5 cl) lemon juice
2 bsp (1 cl) sugar syrup
1 tbsp (1.5 cl) grenadine
cocktail cherries for garnishing

Thoroughly shake the first five ingredients in a shaker
and pour over crushed ice cubes in an Old Fashioned
glass. Garnish with cocktail cherries.

Gin Crusta

Lemon juice and sugar for the rim
2 oz (6 cl) gin
4 bsp (2 cl) lemon juice
4 bsp (2 cl) triple sec
2 bsp (1 cl) maraschino
1 strip lemon peel for garnishing

Moisten the rim of a large tumbler with lemon juice and then dip in sugar. Fill the glass two thirds full with crushed ice. Shake the gin, lemon juice, triple sec, and maraschino in a shaker with ice. Carefully pour into the glass. Serve with a strip of lemon peel and a straw.

Whiskey Crusta

lime juice and brown sugar for the rim
1 cocktail cherry
2 oz (6 cl) Bourbon
4 bsp (2 cl) lime juice
4 bsp (2 cl) sugarcane syrup

Moisten the rim of a large tumbler with lime juice, and then dip in brown sugar. Place a cocktail cherry in the glass and fill it two thirds full with crushed ice. Shake the Bourbon, lime juice, and sugarcane syrup in a shaker with ice. Carefully pour into the glass and serve with a straw.

Refreshing: juleps and smashes

Anybody serving a tray full of juleps at a party need not worry about creating a party atmosphere. Fresh mint and the exotic smoky sweetness of Bourbon add a touch of *Gone with the Wind* and southern states romance to any summer party. The first julep was probably mixed in Virginia in the 18th century, becoming such a cultural asset that it was proudly presented in Washington in the 1850s by a senator named Henry Clay. The word julep allegedly derives from the Arabic *julap* or

the Persian *gulap*, and means rose water. How the term made its way from the Orient into American bar culture remains a mystery, however.

The Mint Julep is still a permanent feature of southern states culture today and is therefore one of the official drinks served at the sophisticated Kentucky Derby, where an astounding 120,000 glasses of the cocktail were ordered in 2007, using more than a ton/tonne of crushed fresh mint. In 2006 guests paid US $1,000 for

American

In 1964 the US Congress declared that

Bourbon
• must be produced in the United States;
• must be made from a grain mixture containing at least 51% corn;
• may not be distilled with an alcohol content exceeding 80% vol;
• must be 100% natural (only water can be added);
• must be aged in new, charred casks made from American white oak.
Straight Bourbon meets these requirements and has been aged for at least two years; if matured less than four years, the age must be indicated on the label.
Rye Whiskey must meet the same requirements, and be made from at least 51% rye.
Wheat Whiskey also has to meet the same requirements and be made from at least 51% wheat.

the luxury version that comprised mint imported from Ireland, Australian sugar, ice from the Bavarian Alps, and a generous shot of Woodford Reserve Bourbon. The profits were used to pay for the upkeep of retired race horses.

The Mint Julep is featured in *The Great Gatsby*, the sociocritical novel by F. Scott Fitzgerald written in 1925, during the American Prohibition. Ray Charles, Homer Simpson, Bob Dylan, and the Beastie Boys have also paid homage to it. Goldfinger sang its praises to James Bond as "very palatable." A native of the southern states, Dr. Leonard Horatio McCoy, played by DeForest Kelley, surgeon on board the spaceship Enterprise, even mixed his favorite drink in space, despite Mister Spock's raising his flexible eyebrows in surprise.

Juleps are always made with freshly crushed mint leaves and then stirred in the glass together with crushed ice, while Bourbon and cane sugar are also usually added. The garnish comprises not fruit but a sprig of mint.

A smash is very similar to a julep, but is prepared in a shaker and can be decorated with a lot of fruit. It also has a shot of soda added to it, making it even more refreshing and therefore all the more suited to daytime summer temperatures.

Whiskey

Corn Whiskey must be distilled from a minimum of 80% corn.
American Light Whiskey is a blend of light grain whiskies that have been distilled at a minimum alcohol content of 80% vol.
Blended Whiskey must contain at least 20% whiskey, blended with neutral, 95% grain spirit.
Tennessee Whiskey is actually a Bourbon, the only differences being that it is filtered in sugar maple charcoal before aging, and may only be produced in that state.

Superb bourbons like Elijah Craig or Evan Williams mature in the rackhouses of the Heaven Hill Distilleries.

Refreshing: juleps and smashes

Tequila Smash

3 kumquats, halved
3 tbsp (5 cl) tequila
1 tbsp (1.5 cl) lime juice
1 tbsp (1.5 cl) maraschino
soda
blueberries for garnishing (optional)

Place the kumquats in a tall glass and crush gently with a pestle. Fill the glass half full with crushed ice. Shake the tequilu, lime juice, and maraschino in a shaker and add to glass, topping up with soda.

A smash comprises a spirit, sugar, soda, and a flavoring ingredient that, due to its kinship with the julep, is usually mint. A sweet liqueur can be used instead of sugar and fruit instead of mint.

Champagne Julep

3 tbsp (4 cl) brandy
1 bsp sugar, mint leaves
champagne
1 sprig mint for garnishing

Place the first three ingredients in a tumbler and gently crush the mint leaves—the mint is only intended to emphasize the freshness of the champagne. Add some crushed ice, top up with champagne, stir briefly, and garnish with a sprig of mint.

Mint Julep

leaves from 1 sprig fresh mint
1 bsp demerara sugar
a little water or dark sugar syrup
2 oz (6 cl) Bourbon
mint leaves for garnishing

Gently crush the mint leaves. Place the first three ingredients in a tumbler, top up with the Bourbon and with crushed ice, stir, and garnish with mint leaves.

Mojito

juice of ½ lime
1 bsp sugar
few mint leaves
½ lime squeezed and cut into quarters
2 oz (6 cl) white rum
soda, 1 sprig of mint

Crush the mint with a pestle. Place the first three ingredients in a tumbler. Add the squeezed lime quarters. Top up with the white rum and crushed ice. Stir and float with a shot of soda. Garnish with a sprig of mint.

Fruity: sangría and cold punches

No Spanish holiday is complete without sangría. However, the high-proof versions that flow along the concrete beaches of the Balearics often do the name no justice. A sangría in Spain is like a Feuerzangenbowle in Germany. You either make it yourself or you don't bother. A Spaniard would never order a glass of sangría in a bar; that is something that only the tourists do. Sangría was originally a soft

Spanish brandy:

Wherever you go in Spain, there is a greeting from a bull. It was devised by the designer Manolo Prieto as an advertisement for Osborne's Brandy Veterano. When the Spanish government condemned advertising boards on freeways in 1988, it took a national furor to save the bull. Unburdened by any logo, it now rises up with pride as the image of Spain and has the highest approval in the land to do so.

Yet the effectiveness of advertising lies in the eye of the beholder, so irrespective of its unparalleled career as a brand name, the bull will continue to be associated with the company from Puerto de Santa Maria, which along with Jerez de la Frontera and Sanlúcar de Barrameda is one of the three sources prescribed by law for Brandy de Jerez. Nine out of ten bottles of brandy come from the "sherry triangle," whose points are marked out by the three aforementioned towns. Sherry itself is also responsible for giving brandy its unique identity, winning the same recognition for Brandy de Jerez as cognac and Armagnac, the official appellation designation as a guarantee of origin among brandies. Unlike those of its French counterparts, the Brandy de Jerez

drink. Wine, and there is plenty of it in Spain, was too much during the heat of the day, and fruit juices are not very popular. Incidentally, the word *sangría* comes from the Spanish term for "bloodletting."

In its original version, all that is added to red wine is an orange and a lemon, two peaches, some sugar, a shot of brandy (optional), and mineral water. These days there are various combinations going by a wide variety of names. *Calimocho* or *pitilingorri*, or else *caliguay* or *rebujito*, all of which are wine combinations with cola, juice, and lemonade. A good sangría is by no means a sign of western decadence, however. Instead, it is a pleasant way of ending a hot summer day with a light drink. Lemonade, sugar, and spirits, enjoyed by holidaymakers as a quick fix, are not among the original ingredients but, used in moderation, they can add an extra touch, especially Spanish brandy.

the mark of the bull and solera

appellation is not related to the origin of the grapes, but to their elaboration. It is so special that it deserves this honor. The brandy must age in casks that have previously contained sherry, so it owes a great deal of its character to sherries, and is dependent on them for the type of aroma they impart to the casks—whether it is a fino, amontillado, oloroso, or Pedro Ximénez. The result is brandies that distinguish themselves by their smoothness and sweetness, or as they are in the habit of saying in Andalusia, "fire on the tongue, velvet in the throat and warmth in the stomach."

BRANDY DE JEREZ: 3 QUALITIES

Solera must age for at least 6 months in casks, but mostly matures for 12.
Solera Reserva must age for at least 12 months in casks, but mostly matures for 30.
Solera Gran Reserva must age for at least 3 years in casks, but often matures for 8, 12, or more years.

Torres in Penedès produces one of the best-known brandies in Spain.

Fruity: sangría and cold punches

Sangría

1–2 tbsp honey according to taste
25 oz (75 cl) red wine (Rioja Crianza)
17 oz (50 cl) orange juice
17 oz (50 cl) red grape juice
1 oz (3 cl) Licor 43 or Spanish brandy
½ organic orange, thinly sliced
½ organic lemon, thinly sliced

½ organic apple, thinly sliced
1¼ lb (500 g) ice cubes

Dissolve the honey in the red wine, orange juice, and grape juice. Add the Licor 43 or Spanish brandy, together with the sliced fruit. Chill for 24 hours. Add the ice cubes before serving.

Sangría Blanca

25 oz (75 cl) dry white wine
8 oz (25 cl) banana juice
8 oz (25 cl) peach juice, 17 oz (50 cl) white grape juice
3 tbsp (5 cl) Cointreau
sliced peaches, bananas, lemons, and kumquats
1¼ lb (500 g) ice cubes

Combine the first five ingredients and add the sliced fruit.
Leave to infuse in the refrigerator for 24 hours. Add the
ice cubes before serving in a large bowl.

Afrococo Punch

Zest of 1 organic lime
2 oz (6 cl) vermouth rosso
17 oz (50 cl) cream
2 cans coconut milk
ground cinnamon and nutmeg
2 pints (100 cl) light rum

Combine the first five ingredients in the list in a saucepan
and slowly bring to the boil; allow to simmer gently for
10 minutes and then let it cool. Top up with the rum,
check the taste, and chill for 2 days. Serve in brandy bal-
loons sprinkled with a little cinnamon.

Beer Punch

2 pints (100 cl) light beer
1 oz (3 cl) sherry
1 oz (3 cl) brandy
2 tbsp confectioner's sugar
ground nutmeg
zest of 1 lemon

Combine the first four ingredients in a bowl. Add some
ice cubes. Garnish with nutmeg and lemon zest.

Fruity: bowls

Fruit is normally used to garnish cocktails and, ideally, it should be esthetic but not over the top, somewhat chic but a secondary detail in most cases. The drinks in this chapter, however, are among the key players. They vary according to the time of year and are ideally suited to summer parties.

The term "bowl" came into use in the 18th century. In addition to an inexpensive sparkling wine, white wine—preferably a very dry one—is used as it offsets the sweetness of the fruit. The fruit is soaked in the white wine the day before and absorbs plenty of alcohol.

The quality ranges from cheap sparkling wine with tinned fruit to fresh fruits of the forest with the finest sparkling wine or champagne. The ingredients are served chilled in a round bowl. In order to keep

Summer in a glass:

Fruit liqueurs now offer a wealth of variety that is unmatched by any other liqueur category. Producers play around skillfully with an amazing range of constituents. Some use only fresh juices, others the extracts of fruits soaked in alcohol. Sometimes these extracts are then distilled to filter out only the finest, purest flavors. Those creating fruit liqueurs also have other ingredients at their fingertips, such as spices, different types of sugar, and of course the base alcohol—which can include fruit spirits as well as neutral alcohol.

While fruit juice liqueurs flaunt the vibrant colors of their fruits, fruit zest liqueurs generally appear clear, or at most slightly tinted. In these products the extracts obtained through maceration, infusion, or percolation are added. Often it is the peels of oranges or other citrus

the liquid cold the entire bowl is placed in a container of ice, or else a glass cylinder containing ice cubes is suspended in the bowl and the refreshing beverage is served on the terrace on summer afternoons.

On the other hand, colorful combinations and a basket full of fruit are all you need to create new ideas. If you like being inventive, then coolers and cobblers are the thing for you. Both come in large glasses with plenty of liquid, attractively decorated with elaborate garnishes.

Coolers are among the most well known of cocktails. The basis spirit and/or a wine-based drink is poured into a tall or highball glass together with ginger ale—according to the original recipe at least—water, or lemonade.

The cobbler is also a generous drink served with crushed ice, but is mixed with wine, liqueur, fruit, juice, or syrup in a highball glass. Cobblers are famous for their attractive, elaborate garnishes. There are those who say that cobblers are like a fruit salad, just with alcohol and for drinking.

fruit liqueurs

fruits that give their bittersweet flavor to this type of liqueur. One of the best-loved classics among the fruit zest liqueurs is curaçao, with its deep blue color. A centuries-old Dutch invention, it is now produced by many different companies.

Normally fruit liqueurs are served neat and chilled, or with juice, seltzer, or sodas as a long drink. In the past they were mixed only with champagne and dry white wine, but their qualities when combined with other spirits have been appreciated for a long time—they certainly add delightful fruity notes to cocktails. Incidentally, fruit juice liqueurs have a sensitive reaction to oxygen, so lengthy storage is not appropriate. But of course it does not necessarily have to come to that…

Fruity: bowls

Balaclava

25 oz (75 cl) red Bordeaux
1 cucumber, thinly sliced
juice of 2 lemons
5 bsp (2.5 cl) sugar syrup
½ organic lemon, thinly pared
a few lemon balm leaves
1 block of ice made from about 2 pints (1 liter) water
25 oz (75 cl) mineral water
25 oz (75 cl) sparkling wine

Combine the first four ingredients in a bowl. Suspend a
sieve containing the lemon peel and the lemon balm
in the bowl and leave to infuse in the refrigerator for
1 hour. Remove the sieve. Add the block of ice to chill it,
and add the mineral water and sparkling wine.

Pineapple Cooler

25 oz (75 cl) Sauternes or a similar sweet white wine
juice of 1 lemon
8 oz (25 cl) pineapple juice
1 oz (3 cl) sugar syrup
9 oz (250 g) pineapple pieces
dry sparkling wine

Combine the first five ingredients and leave to infuse in
the refrigerator overnight. Top up with chilled dry
sparkling wine the next day.

Rose Bowl

....

petals of 5 scented roses
sugar
25 oz (75 cl) dry Riesling
1 ice block made from
approx. 2 pints (1 liter) water
25 oz (75 cl) dry sparkling wine, well chilled

Place the rose petals in a bowl, sprinkle with sugar, and crush gently. Add the Riesling. Leave to infuse at room temperature for 2 hours, add the block of ice to chill, and add the dry sparkling wine.

Fruits of the Forest Bowl

....

2 lb (1 kg) fruits of the forest (wild strawberries, black-berries, raspberries, blueberries, blackcurrants), small berries pierced, large berries halved
2 white peaches, peeled, pits removed, and finely diced
sugar
50 oz (150 cl) dry Riesling
1 ice block made from approx.
2 pints (1 liter) water
25 oz (75 cl) sparkling wine

Layer the fruit in a bowl and sprinkle with sugar. Add 25 oz (75 cl) Riesling and leave to infuse in the refrigerator overnight. Chill the bowl with the ice block, add the remaining Riesling, and top up with the sparkling wine.

Fruity: coolers and cobblers

Springtime Cooler

3 tbsp (4 cl) vodka
4 bsp (2 cl) triple sec
2 oz (6 cl) orange juice
1 oz (3 cl) lemon juice
2 bsp (1 cl) sugar syrup
fruit for garnishing, e.g. star fruit, Cape gooseberries
cocktail cherries for garnishing

Shake the first five ingredients in a shaker with ice and
filter into a long glass of crushed ice. Garnish with fruit
and cocktail cherries.

Starfish Cooler

3 orange slices , 12 mint leaves
4 bsp (2 cl) Limoncello, 4 bsp (2 cl) grenadine
4 bsp (2 cl) unsweetened iced tea
2 bsp (1 cl) sugar syrup
champagne

Gently crush the orange slices and mint leaves in an Old
Fashioned glass. Add the Limoncello, grenadine, iced tea,
and sugar syrup, and top up with crushed ice. Stir and
float with a generous splash of champagne.

In 2007 the bartender Stacy Smith won the annual Tales
of the Cocktail bartenders' competition in New Orleans
with this drink.

Rum Cobbler

2 oz (6 cl) rum
4 bsp (2 cl) sugar syrup
mixed fruit, e.g. pineapple, green grapes, strawberries,
kiwi fruit, mango, orange, etc.

Prepare the fruit and cut into small pieces. Fill a large,
tall glass with crushed ice. Add the rum and sugar syrup,
followed by the fruit. Carefully mix a few pieces of fruit
into the top layer of ice. Serve with a straw and a
teaspoon.

Coco Cobbler

3 tbsp (4 cl) dark rum
2 bsp (1 cl) dark tequila
1 oz (3 cl) Batida de Côco
2 bsp (1 cl) amaretto
2 oz (6 cl) orange juice
1 oz (3 cl) lime juice
3 tbsp (4 cl) apple juice
fruit for garnishing

Fill a tall glass with shaved ice.
Shake all of the main ingredients together in a shaker.
Filter into the tall glass and garnish generously with
suitable fruit.

Tropical: daiquiris

Four out of five of the mixed drinks ordered at your average bar are tropicals. That was not always the case, however, with the drinks usually ordered being dry and strongly alcoholic. It was the bar renaissance of the 1990s that opened the way to the top of the menu for tropical drinks. Tropical drinks are precisely the opposite of their predecessors and cover a wide range of flavors. They can be combined with many liqueurs and other modifiers, even cream (Piña Colada). And almost all of them are ideally suited to softening the taste of the high-proof alcohol. They also harmonize well with lively local spirits such as rum, cachaça, and tequila. Tropical drinks are intensely flavored but seldom taste of alcohol. This is the secret of their success and, for those who neither want to taste nor to drink alcohol, there is the option of an alcohol-free mocktail. One of the most popular tropical drinks is the daiquiri, allegedly invented by the American engineer Jennings Cox. The gin ran out prior to a reception at the place where he was working in Cuba, the Daiquirí mine, near Santiago de Cuba. Desperate, he used white rum and limes.

The daiquiri achieved international fame through Ernest Hemingway, who consumed vast quantities of the drink and sometimes tried out different versions. Some of these are still in existence, such as the Hemingway Special, for example, the Daiquiri Floridita, and the Papas Daiquiri with double the amount of rum for the hard drinking macho. This Caribbean drink went on to become truly American with John F. Kennedy declaring it his favorite aperitif. Marlene Dietrich used to order it when on tour in Europe, and John Cazale alias Fredo Corleone ordered it in *The Godfather*.

Ernest Hemingway was a regular patron of the Floridita bar, famed for its daiquiris.

Rum STRONG STUFF FROM THE CARIBBEAN

Sugarcane: the raw material for rum

Steam engines crush the canes.

Weak sugarcane wine

Rum is distilled in columns.

Today as always, the old steam engine on Martinique is still used to power shredders and mills that divest the tough sugarcane of its fibers and break it down. Stream water flows in to allow the sugar to be extracted better. This juice is filtered and pumped into open tanks, combined with yeast, and stocked in vats. In 24 to 72 hours it ferments and becomes *vin de canne*, the 3.5–6% by volume alcohol sugarcane wine that can be distilled.

The copper distillation apparatus typical of the Antilles consists of a tall column divided into 15 to 20 levels. The preheated sugarcane wine is fed up through the column. On the way from top to bottom it passes through the various levels, being sprayed through a metal bell on each level. At the bottom vapor is introduced into the column. Where wine and vapor encounter one another, a violent, continuous bubbling takes place. Gradually the vapor becomes laden with volatile components—alcohol, ester, aldehyde. Thus enriched, it makes its way up to the top of the column, from where it is fed through the swan neck and the chauffe-vin which it heats, and into the condenser. Here it cools and liquefies, and is collected as clear rum with an alcohol content of 65–75% by volume.

Tropical: daiquiris

Daiquiri Floridita

3 tbsp (4 cl) white rum
4 bsp (2 cl) lime juice
4 bsp (2 cl) maraschino
1 bsp sugar syrup

Thoroughly shake all of the ingredients in a shaker and filter into a cocktail glass.

Ernest Hemingway's favorite bartender in Havana, Constante, mixed this drink for the writer in the El Floridita bar. A slight modification with a dash of grapefruit juices turns it into a Hemingway Special.

Illusion

3 tbsp (4 cl) rum
4 bsp (2 cl) melon liqueur
4 bsp (2 cl) orange liqueur
4 bsp (2 cl) lemon juice
3 tbsp (4 cl) passion fruit juice

Thoroughly shake all of the ingredients in a shaker and filter into a cocktail glass. Serve with a toothpick and a piece of fruit. If you are clever with your hands you will be able to make an accomplished impression.

Mango Daiquiri

3 tbsp (4 cl) mango puree
4 bsp (2 cl) lime juice
4 bsp (2 cl) sugar syrup
3 tbsp (5 cl) white rum
mango wedges for garnishing

Place the first four ingredients in an electric mixer together with some ice cubes. Puree and pour into a cocktail glass. Garnish with mango wedges.

Strawberry Daiquiri

1 handful of strawberries
1 handful of ice cubes
juice of ¼ lime
1 bsp sugar syrup
3 tbsp (5 cl) white rum
2 bsp (1 cl) strawberry syrup
½ strawberry for garnishing

Place all the main ingredients in an electric mixer. Mix until smooth and serve in a large cocktail glass. Garnish with a half strawberry.

Tropical: sunrises

Apple Sunrise

4 bsp (2 cl) cassis
5 tbsp (8 cl) orange juice
3 tbsp (4 cl) Calvados
2 bsp (1 cl) lemon juice
apple wedge and blackcurrants for garnishing

Stir the cassis and orange juice with ice cubes individually in a separate mixing glass. Pour into a tall glass in layers. Using a pair of tongs, carefully add some more ice cubes. Top up with the Calvados and the lemon juice. Garnish with an apple wedge and blackcurrants on the rim.

Tequila Sunrise

juice of ½ lime
3 tbsp (5 cl) tequila
3 oz (10 cl) orange juice , 1 shot grenadine

Fill a tall glass two thirds full with crushed ice. Add the lime juice, tequila, and orange juice and stir; then float with a shot of grenadine.

The mother of all sunrises has the advantage that it is in the glass in no time at all. The main thing is that the grenadine creates a few bright red streaks through the orange juice.

Barbados Sunrise

2 oz (6 cl) dark rum—from Barbados, of course
2 oz (6 cl) orange juice
3 tbsp (5 cl) passion fruit juice
1 oz (3 cl) lime juice
4 bsp (2 cl) grenadine
pineapple slices and mint for garnishing

Thoroughly shake the first four ingredients in a shaker
with ice and filter into a glass with fresh ice cubes.
Carefully add the grenadine. Garnish with pineapple
slices and mint.

Brazilian Sunrise

3 tbsp (4 cl) cachaça
2 bsp (1 cl) lemon juice
3 oz (10 cl) orange juice
4 bsp (2 cl) grenadine

Thoroughly shake the first three ingredients in a shaker
with ice cubes and filter into a tall glass with crushed ice.
Add the grenadine in a fine stream.

Ideally, the syrup mixes with the upper half of the drink,
causing the colors to run slightly: that's sunset on the
Copacabana Beach.

Tropical: margaritas and coladas

Salt, citrus fruit, and the bitter sweet orange aroma—just a touch, mind you—and everything ice cold! More than almost any other drink, the margarita embodies the subtle magic that a mixed drink can create: complex but harmonious, cool and hot at the same time. The margarita is one of the best drinks in the world, as well as one of the most famous. It is therefore no wonder that the list of self-proclaimed originators resembles a small town telephone directory.

The most well known must be the German, Danny Negrete, who roamed around Mexico as a restaurateur from 1936 to 1944, falling in love with a señorita named Margarita in the process. She had a penchant for salty drinks, which is why he invented the margarita just for her. A nice idea and a nice story that is told often but will probably never be proven.

Enrique Bastante Gutierez was more successful with his story, claiming to have invented the margarita for the actress Margarita Carmen Cansino. In order to understand what makes this version of how the margarita came about so interesting, you need to know that the star's stage name was Rita Hayworth.

The colada has virtually become a synonym for Caribbean drinks. Coconut, pineapple juice, and cream are the typical components, but these can vary as almost anything from raspberries to pineapple, from coffee to chocolate, goes with a colada.

Coconut cream is obtained from the first pressing of fresh coconut shavings and has a fat content of some 35%. Coconut milk, a combination of coconut cream and the liquid obtained from the second pressing of the same coconut shavings, thinned with a little water, contains only 10–20% fat. The fat content is the deciding factor.

The *Washington Post* made mention of a refreshing pineapple drink named Piña Fría as early as 1906. Rum and coconut were only added later. The title of inventor has many pretenders and the number of Caribbean bartenders claiming to have invented the colada has continued to grow since the 1950s. It goes without saying that a pineapple and coconut ice cream dessert named Pina Colada Ice Cream, which was already being praised in American newspapers as early as the 1930s, remains a favorite today.

The moderately successful composer Rupert Holmes landed an evergreen hit with *Escape*, better known as the *Piña Colada Song*, which made it to the top of the charts when it was released in 1980.

How to drink tequila

Slightly dampen the back of the hand, sprinkle some sea salt on it, lick off the salt, bite into a piece of lime, then swallow the tequila, or vice versa. This is how tequila, as a shot in pubs and discos, became a cult drink, but strict rituals are generally only practiced in certain friendly cliques. Some also like oranges and cinnamon, and drop into the glass a coffee bean that they then crunch up to finish. A typical routine is a two-handed one, with a tequila in one hand and a Sangrita, a sharp Mexican juice cocktail, in the other, a combination originating from the Tequila region.

Tropical: margaritas

Cassis Margarita

blue curaçao
sugar
2 oz (6 cl) tequila
1–1½ oz (3–4 cl) cassis
4 bsp (2 cl) lemon juice
fresh fruit for garnishing

Dip the rim of the margarita glass in a saucer of blue curaçao and then in sugar. Shake the rest of the ingredients in a shaker with ice and carefully filter into the glass. Garnish with plenty of fresh fruit on a toothpick.

The sugared rim is primarily for decoration and may be omitted.

Margarita

1 lemon wedge
fine salt
2 oz (6 cl) tequila reposado
3 tbsp (4 cl) triple sec
4 bsp (2 cl) lemon juice

Moisten the rim of a margarita glass with the lemon wedge and dip in some fine salt. Carefully shake off the loose salt grains. Thoroughly shake the remaining ingredients in a shaker with crushed ice. Carefully filter into the glass.
The salted rim is the hallmark of the margarita but is nevertheless a matter of dispute. Many bartenders will tell you on the side that the salt can conceal a lesser quality tequila.

Frozen Mango Margarita

2 oz (6 cl) mango juice
2 oz (6 cl) tequila
4 bsp (2 cl) lime juice
2 bsp (1 cl) mango syrup
star fruit and redcurrants for garnishing

Place all the main ingredients in an electric mixer. Half
fill with ice cubes and mix until you have a sorbet-like
consistency. Pour into a margarita glass, and garnish with
star fruit and redcurrants.

Banana Margarita

1 ripe banana, peeled
2 oz (6 cl) tequila
1 oz (3 cl) Galliano
4 bsp (2 cl) lime juice
slices of citrus fruit for garnishing

Place all the main ingredients in an electric mixer. Half
fill with ice cubes and mix until you have a smooth liquid.
Filter into a margarita glass and garnish with slices of
citrus fruit, or other fruit.

Tropical: coladas

Choco Colada

4 bsp (2 cl) dark rum
4 bsp (2 cl) white rum
1 tbsp (1.5 cl) Tia Maria
4 bsp (2 cl) crème de cacao
2 bsp (1 cl) coconut cream
3 tbsp (5 cl) cream
dark chocolate and banana slices for garnishing

Thoroughly shake all the main ingredients in a shaker, and filter into a large tumbler of crushed ice. Grate the dark chocolate over the top and garnish with slices of banana.

Apricot Colada

3 tbsp (5 cl) white rum
2 bsp (1 cl) apricot brandy
2 oz (6 cl) apricot juice
4 bsp (2 cl) pineapple juice
3 tbsp (4 cl) coconut cream
2 bsp (1 cl) crème de cacao
apricots and pineapples for garnishing

Thoroughly shake all the main ingredients in a shaker, and filter into a large beaker of crushed ice. Garnish with apricots and pineapple.

Piña Colada

3 tbsp (4 cl) coconut cream
2 oz (6 cl) fresh pineapple juice
1 oz (3 cl) dark rum
1 oz (3 cl) white rum
1 wedge pineapple, 1 piece coconut, 1 cocktail cherry for garnishing

Place the first four ingredients in an electric mixer and mix until you have a smooth liquid. Pour into a tall, wide glass and garnish with the pineapple wedge, coconut, and cocktail cherry.

French Colada

4 bsp (2 cl) white rum
2 bsp (1 cl) cognac
2 bsp (1 cl) cassis
1 oz (3 cl) pineapple juice
2 bsp (1 cl) coconut cream
4 bsp (2 cl) cream
Cape gooseberries (for example) for garnishing

Thoroughly shake all the main ingredients in a shaker, and filter into a large cocktail glass of crushed ice. Garnish with a Cape gooseberry or other fruit.

Tropical: Caribbean punches and swizzles

Punch can be both a hot drink and a tropical drink with lots of fruit. The word punch comes from the Hindi *panch* and means five, referring to the original ingredients: arrack, sugar, lemon, water, and tea. The sailors of the British East India Company brought the word to Europe, and the first mention of the word in British documents was in 1632. Initially they were largely hot winter punches, but the first Jamaica Punch had already become popular by 1655. Punch houses came into existence just 20 years later.

The most famous punch is most certainly the planter's punch, even though it does not constitute a specific mixture. It refers to a mixed drink with a rum base and diverse tropical fruits and fruit juices.

Just as well known is the mai tai, the invention of which is a matter of dispute between the American gastro-legends Trader Vic's and Donn Beach. The punch owes its name to Thai guests to whom it was served and who expressed their satisfaction with mai tai, meaning "tastes good."

The swizzle's namesake is the swizzle stick, the little mixing stick for mixed drinks that has acquired two teeth. Its history began in 1934. Shortly after the end of the Prohibition, Jack Sindler was sitting in Boston's Ritz Carlton Hotel, trying unsuccessfully to fish the olive out of his martini. The inventor immediately had the idea of perfecting the hunt with a small harpoon and had the swizzle stick patented.

There were some rum drinks known as swizzles in the 19th century, however, possibly relating to the colloquial meaning of swizzler: a swindler. The Swizzle Inn in the Bermuda Islands is famous for its swizzles, which it promotes with the fitting slogan "Swizzle Inn, swagger out."

Cachaça BRAZIL'S NATIONAL DRINK

Firstly the sugarcane is crushed,

The juice is diluted with water and fermented,

then distilled in alembics.

and matured in wooden barrels.

Neat or as Caipirinha with lime, sugar, and ice—cachaça is, without contest, Brazil's national drink. Around 30,000 producers supply the market, including some major industrial firms, but the almost 5,000 brands on the market predominantly originate in small and sometimes tiny distilleries. More than 340 million gallons (1.3 billion liters) per year are produced, making cachaça the third major spirit in the world in terms of quantity, after vodka and soju. Only 1% of it, a paltry 3.4 million gallons (13 million liters), is exported. The Brazilians drink their cachaça themselves. Their folk drink has a long tradition, even if it has been fashionable only since the 1990s.

As cachaça is based on fresh sugarcane, its aromas—reminiscent of blossom, exotic fruits, and honey—also give it its distinctive profile. The better the distillation, the finer its expression.

Cachaças from the famous regions of Pernambuco and Minas have a very good reputation. Golden, amber, or golden brown cachaça is matured in wood and now has cult status. Particularly fine are the clear cachaças matured in wood that does not give off its color, such as Jequitibá rosa. The Bavarian-based company "Caipiu one world drink" bottles and markets premium artisanal organic cachaças made by a number of small-scale producers.

Tropical: Caribbean punches and swizzles

Zombie

1 oz (3 cl) white rum
2 oz (6 cl) dark rum
1 bsp sugar syrup
4 bsp (2 cl) lime juice
1 oz (3 cl) pineapple juice
1 bsp apricot brandy
1 dash pastis
1 dash angostura
mint and fruit for garnishing

Shake all the main ingredients in a cold shaker and filter into a large glass of crushed ice. Garnish with mint and fruit.

Rum Punch

3 tbsp (5 cl) white rum
2 bsp (1 cl) orange curaçao
3 tbsp (4 cl) passion fruit juice
2 bsp (1 cl) amaretto
4 bsp (2 cl) lemon juice, 1 bsp sugar syrup
½ passion fruit for garnishing (optional)

Thoroughly shake all the main ingredients in a shaker.
Filter into a beaker of crushed ice. You can garnish the
Rum Punch with a half passion fruit.

Mai Tai

3 tbsp (5 cl) dark rum
1 oz (3 cl) white rum
juice of 1 lime, 1 oz (3 cl) grapefruit juice
2 bsp (1 cl) vanilla syrup, 2 bsp (1 cl) orange curaçao
2 bsp (1 cl) canesugar syrup
2 dashes angostura, mint and pineapple for garnishing

Thoroughly shake all the main ingredients in a shaker,
and filter into a beaker of shaved ice. Garnish with mint
and pineapple.

Ti' Punch

½ lemon
2 bsp (1 cl) canesugar syrup
2 oz (6 cl) rum

Squeeze the lemon and place the zest in a beaker. Stir in
the cane-sugar syrup and the rum.

Ti ' punch (short for Petit Punch) is served as an aperitif
on the French-speaking islands of the Caribbean.

Tropical: cachaça drinks

Brazilian Crush

4–5 kumquats
2 oz (6 cl) cachaça
1 tbsp (1.5 cl) grenadine
2 bsp (1 cl) lime juice
sprig of mint and a straw for garnishing

Halve the kumquats and crush gently in a tumbler with a pestle. Add some crushed ice and mix well with the kumquats. Thoroughly shake the remaining ingredients in a shaker, filter into the glass, stir briefly, and garnish with a sprig of mint and a straw.

Batida de Côco

1 small, ripe banana
3 tbsp (5 cl) pineapple juice
4 bsp (2 cl) cream
4 bsp (2 cl) coconut cream
3 tbsp (5 cl) cachaça
pineapple for garnishing

Mix all the main ingredients in an electric mixer until the banana is pureed. Fill a tall glass three quarters full with crushed ice, pour in the Batida and stir. Garnish with pineapple.

Caipirinha

1 organic lime, cut into pieces
2 bsp demerara sugar
2 oz (6 cl) cachaça

Place the lime pieces and the sugar in a thick-bottomed tumbler. Squeeze the juice out of the lime pieces using a pestle. Add the cachaça, stir, and top up with crushed ice. Stir again briefly.

Copacabana at Dawn

2 oz (6 cl) cachaça
3 tbsp (5 cl) passion fruit juice
4 bsp (2 cl) chocolate syrup
1 oz (3 cl) cream, slice of star fruit for garnishing

Thoroughly shake all the main ingredients in a shaker and filter into a tall glass containing ice cubes. Garnish with a slice of star fruit.

Chocolate and passion fruit are ideal partners. In the right proportions they develop a sophisticated, bitter-exotic aroma.

Tropical: mocktails with a dash

Aperol Starter

3 tsp (4 cl) Aperol
1 oz (3 cl) orange juice
2 bsp (1 cl) canesugar syrup
4 bsp (2 cl) lime cordial
2 bsp (1 cl) lime juice
1 cocktail cherry for garnishing

Shake all the main ingredients in a shaker and filter into a narrow goblet with ice cubes; garnish with a cocktail cherry.

A pleasant, straightforward, light, bitter aperitif.

Golden Cadillac Convertible

4 bsp (2 cl) white crème de cacao
2 bsp (1 cl) vanilla syrup
3 tsp (4 cl) orange juice
4 bsp (2 cl) cream
1 kumquat for garnishing

Shake all the main ingredients together well in a shaker. Filter into a cocktail glass and garnish with a kumquat. This mocktail is a clever modification of the Golden Cadillac, with the Galliano replaced with vanilla syrup.

Mojito Mocktail

1 sprig of mint
1–2 bsp demerara sugar
2 drops angostura
soda water
1 sprig of mint for garnishing

Remove the leaves from the sprig of mint and place in a tumbler together with the demerara sugar and angostura. Crush the leaves gently using a pestle. Fill the glass with crushed ice, top up with soda water, stir briefly, and garnish with the second sprig of mint.

Colada Linda

1 oz (3 cl) Batida de Côco
1 oz (3 cl) coconut cream
2 oz (6 cl) pineapple juice
4 bsp (2 cl) cream
2 bsp (1 cl) canesugar syrup
piece of pineapple for garnishing

Place all the main ingredients in an electric mixer together with a handful of ice cubes. Mix until you have a smooth mixture and pour into a tall glass. Serve with a straw and garnished with a piece of pineapple on the rim of the glass.

Whimsical: molecular drinks

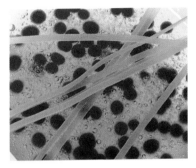

A little creativity in the combination of aromas and fruit should be invested in every drink. The cocktails on the following pages are for those that like experimenting and that can handle intelligently composed drinks with surprising ingredients.

Mocha foam and encapsulated pulpo pearls have created a stir in haute cuisine. Ferran Adrià, the Spanish protagonist of molecular cuisine, has managed to change foodstuffs through the addition of neutral chemicals to such an extent that they attain a completely new consistency. Algae turn into lollies and lobster transforms into foam (*espuma*).

Resourceful bar mixers already have molecular cocktails in their repertoires. Whiskey Sour with *espuma de maracuya* and Bloody Mary with "celery pearls" are ideally suited to perplexing the evening's guests. Cocktails are broken down into gels

and droplets that explode in the guest's mouth, guaranteeing surprised reactions.

Anybody who wants to mix molecular drinks themselves needs to acquire an assortment of chemicals first of all. Gelling and thickening agents made from algae, seaweed, vegetable fibers, or seeds, in particular, are required. The calcium lactate required for making gel capsules is an organic mineral compound. These are therefore natural products, colorless and neutral in flavor. One or other of the ingredients may be somewhat pricey but, in general, they are not exorbitantly expensive.

That also applies to the hardware requirements: bowls and a high-speed mixer, perhaps a precision scale, and a couple of other utensils. The inexperienced will need to be prepared to undertake a number of test runs. It is all a question of the precise mixture and the timing. No one product is the same as the next. Even a syrup from two different manufacturers requires different quantities.

Quick success can be achieved with caviar made from Campari, for example. The recipes are intended as practice for beginners that can be elaborated upon as you wish once you have some experience. The precise quantities apply only when using exactly the same products, however.

Whimsical: spicy drinks and fancies

SPICY DRINKS

There are some cocktails whose histories sound like the family sagas of an American oil dynasty, with the family tree going back some 100 or 200 years. Some of them obviously landed in America with the first English ships. Many of those that followed were merely modifications of the earlier versions, with very few of them being truly new, and that includes spicy drinks. They have nothing to do with the usual character tests à la sangrita and Tabasco & Co. Spicy drinks combine typical cocktail ingredients such as spirits, fruit, and liqueurs with aromatic flavorings such as basil, black pepper, and ginger. Their exotic spiciness makes a surprising match for the classic partners. Spicy drinks are among the most interesting of what bar culture has produced this century.

FANCIES

No set recipe, no rules, lots of fruit juice, and imagination, and the fancy drink is ready. Anything goes here. Fancy is everything that doesn't fit into any other category and is preferably bright and colorful. They can vacillate between a long drink and a milkshake, between a tropical cooler and fruit salad. Anything goes, including colored glasses and chunky fruit skewers. The bartender's favorites are therefore seldom missing from any good menu.

Whimsical: molecular drinks

False Cappuccino

3 level bsp xanthazoon, 17 oz (50 cl) Dooleys Cream Liqueur, 2 whipped cream chargers, 3 tbsp (4 cl) Kahlúa, 3 tbsp (4 cl) brandy, Chocolate for garnishing. Equipment: small cream whipper (iSi Whip). Dissolve the xanthazoon in the Dooleys Cream Liqueur, pour into a small cream whipper (iSi Whip), and screw on 2 whipped cream chargers. Leave to chill in the refrigerator for a couple of hours. Prior to serving, shake the Kahlúa with the brandy and some ice in a shaker, filter into a glass, and squirt the Cream Liqueur foam on top. Garnish with fancy chocolate decorations.

Kir Moleculaire

27 oz (80 cl) blackcurrant juice, 4 bsp (2 cl) crème de cassis, 4 bsp (2 cl) lime syrup, pinch (1 g) alginate, 5 level bsp calazoon, 13 cl (2.5 g) calcic. Equipment: syringe. Combine the blackcurrant juice, crème de cassis, and lime syrup. Trickle in the alginate and stir until smooth, taking care to avoid bubbles forming. Leave to stand overnight. Dissolve the calazoon and calcic in 17 oz (50 cl) of cold water. Using a syringe, drizzle the juice and alginate solution into the calcium lactate solution so that caviar-like droplets are formed. Wait 30 seconds for the gel coating to form. Remove the droplets with a skimmer and neutralize them by dipping briefly in cold water. Add the cassis-caviar to a glass of champagne.

Molecular Bloody Mary

6 level bsp guarzoon, 7 oz (20 cl) tomato juice, 7 oz (20 cl) vodka, celery leaves or other kitchen herbs, 1 bsp algizoon, salt, 5 level bsp calazoon. Equipment: syringe. Completely dissolve half the guarzoon in the tomato juice, and half in the vodka. Extract the juice from celery leaves or other kitchen herbs to obtain 3 oz (10 cl) juice. Stir the algizoon into the juice, season lightly with salt, and take care to avoid bubbles forming (best prepared the day before). To serve, fill a large cocktail glass half full with the tomato mixture and leave to set. Add the vodka mixture and again leave to set. Completely dissolve the calazoon in cold water and put aside in a bowl. Prepare a further bowl of water. Place the herb juice in a syringe and drizzle or slowly inject into the calazoon mixture so that long noodles or lentils are formed. Fish them out after 1 minute and rinse in cold water. Place the celery or herb lentils/noodles on the drink. When the guest stirs the drink with a straw, the tomato juice and vodka liquefy and combine. The lentils or noodles burst on the tongue, releasing the flavors.

Piña Colada Espuma

6 leaves of gelatin (each 1/20 oz/1.7 g), 20 oz (60 cl) pineapple juice, 12 oz (35 cl) coconut milk, 3 tbsp (5 cl) dark rum (35% vol. alcohol content), 2 iSi whipped cream chargers, candied fruit for garnishing. Equipment: cream whipper (iSi Whip). Soften the gelatin in cold water, heat some of the pineapple juice, and dissolve the drained gelatin in it. Then combine with the rest of the pineapple juice, the coconut milk, and the rum. Place the liquid in a cream whipper (iSi Whip) and screw on two iSi whipped cream chargers. Leave to chill in the refrigerator for several hours. Before removing, turn the container upside down and shake thoroughly. Squirt into a goblet and garnish with pieces of candied fruit according to taste. Serve with a wide straw and a spoon.

Whimsical: spicy drinks

Green Cucumber

1 piece cucumber
1 piece chili
1 oz (3 cl) gin
1 tbsp (1.5 cl) melon liqueur
1 tbsp (1.5 cl) lime juice
1 tbsp (1.5 cl) canesugar syrup
fresh cucumber and chili for garnishing

Crush the pieces of cucumber and chili in a shaker glass with a pestle. Add the remaining main ingredients, shake thoroughly in the shaker, and filter into a cocktail glass. Garnish with fresh cucumber and chili.

Basil Crush

1 sprig basil
1 oz (3 cl) lime juice
3 tbsp (5 cl) gin
1 tbsp (1.5 cl) canesugar syrup
1 oz (3 cl) cloudy apple juice
basil leaves and lime peel for garnishing

Remove the basil leaves and carefully crush them with a pestle on the base of a tumbler. Thoroughly shake the remaining main ingredients in a shaker. Filter into the tumbler with crushed ice, stir, and garnish with basil leaves and lime peel. Serve with a straw.

Ginger Cosmopolitan

1 oz (3 cl) vodka
2 bsp (1 cl) Cointreau
1 tbsp (1.5 cl) lime juice
3 tbsp (4 cl) cranberry juice
2 bsp (1 cl) ginger liqueur or syrup, or a little freshly
grated ginger
lime, a cocktail cherry, and mint for garnishing

Thoroughly shake all the main ingredients in a shaker,
filter into a cocktail glass, and garnish with lime, a
cocktail cherry, and mint.

Pepper Martini

3 tbsp (4 cl) pepper vodka
2 bsp (1 cl) Noilly Prat
1 tbsp (1.5 cl) Mangalore
chili liqueur
2 red chilies for garnishing

Combine the first four ingredients in a mixing glass with
ice cubes, and stir until the glass is frosted on the
outside. Filter into a martini glass and garnish with the
tips of 2 red chilies.

Whimsical: fancies

Pink Elephant

1 oz (3 cl) Baileys
1 oz (3 cl) strawberry syrup
3 tbsp (4 cl) pineapple juice
3 tbsp (4 cl) passion fruit juice
3 tbsp (4 cl) cream
strawberries and other fruit for garnishing

Shake all the main ingredients in a shaker with ice cubes.
Filter into a fancy glass with ice cubes. Garnish with
strawberries and other fruit.

Vanilla Sky

3 tbsp (4 cl) Vanilla Sky vodka
4 bsp (2 cl) strawberry liqueur
2 bsp (1 cl) vanilla syrup
4 bsp (2 cl) lime juice
3 tbsp (5 cl) cranberry juice
1 oz (3 cl) passion fruit juice
1 pinch nutmeg
fruit, citrus peel, vanilla pod, and 1 sprig mint for
garnishing

Thoroughly shake all the main ingredients in a shaker,
filter into an Old Fashioned glass with crushed ice.
Garnish generously.

Passione

1 oz (3 cl) Malibu
1 oz (3 cl) Passoa
juice of ½ lime
2 oz (6 cl) pineapple juice
3 oz (8 cl) passion fruit juice
strips of orange peel and ½ passion fruit for garnishing

Shake all the main ingredients in a shaker with ice cubes.
Filter into a large brandy balloon with crushed ice.
Garnish with generous strips of orange peel and passion
fruit.

Peppermint Patty

1 oz (3 cl) Captain Morgan spiced Rum
4 bsp (2 cl) Licor 43
3 oz (8 cl) stracciatella (chocolate chip) yogurt
3 tbsp (4 cl) coconut cream
1 oz (3 cl) passion fruit juice
mint and fruit for garnishing

Thoroughly shake all the main ingredients in a shaker.
Pour into a large beaker. Garnish with mint and fruit.

Invigorating: flips

Anybody that drinks a cocktail during the day usually has a good reason for doing so: perhaps a birthday, a promotion, or a hangover from the night before. All of these reasons are justified and each has the drink to match. Most of these drinks tend to have more moderate alcohol con-tent, as well as ingredients such as cream or flavorings that bear some resemblance to the category "foodstuffs." The reasons are obvious: not everyone wants to have to worry about the alcohol levels in their blood in the morning. Flips and eggnogs contain egg yolk, often cream, as well

Port and

Port's reductive style with the appealing fresh sweet cherry and berry fruit continues to attract more and more fans who prize the ruby reserve, late bottled vintage, single quinta vintage, and of course the vintage—the first two have the advantage of being more affordable and more accessible when young, of not needing to be decanted, and of being available in most bars.

Yet the tawnies, the wines matured oxidatively in old barrels, the pipes, are in no way a thing of the past, quite the contrary. The tawnies are still very appealing wines that, with increasing age, often develop a fascinating diversity of aromas often exceeding that of the vintages. The 30- and 40-year-olds, in particular, exhibit a tempting elegance and sophistication seldom found in other wines and spirits.

Immortalized on "azulejos," painted, glazed and hard-fired ceramic tiles: old vineyard terraces near Pinhão

as winter ingredients such as almonds, sherry, and nutmeg. In the USA and other countries they have long been the drinks traditionally served in the winter and at Christmas. Many of them are alcohol free and therefore prepared in large quantities to be drunk by the whole family. The pick-me-ups, on the other hand, contain alcohol and are based on the hair of the dog theory, according to which a small dose of alcohol helps cure a hangover.

One thing that does belong in a flip is egg, together with the base spirit and sugar, and possibly a liqueur. Everything is thoroughly shaken so that the rather viscous ingredients mix well with one another and with the fortified wines such as sherry and port. It also takes longer to chill everything. Nutmeg goes with most of the drinks as decoration. Many flips also contain milk and cream and are then called eggnogs, these having a somewhat higher nutritional value.

Sherry

Sherry presents itself in a variety of styles and qualities. First of all there is the fresh, dry, fortified fino or manzanilla wine. The residents of the sherry triangle have their ancestral brand that they swear by, this often being dictated less by taste and quality and more by sentimental attachment. Ultimately almost everyone has relatives or friends working for one of the sherry producers. The size of a brand is no indication of its quality, smaller producers in

principle not being any better than a worldwide distributor, and vice versa.

Finos and manzanillas, the lightest dry sherries, are universally popular as an aperitif and make the ideal partner for tapas. Well-aged amontillados, palo cortados, and olorosos are a matter for connoisseurs because you need to take your time in order to be able to appreciate fully their world of aromas and structure.

The best locations in the Jerez sherry region have white chalk soils known as albarizas.

Invigorating: flips

Brandy Flip

1 egg yolk
3 tbsp (5 cl) brandy
1 oz (2.5 cl) cream
2 bsp (1 cl) sugar syrup
ground nutmeg for decorating

Thoroughly shake all the main ingredients in a shaker and serve in a cocktail glass, sprinkled with ground nutmeg.

Sherry Flip

1 egg yolk
3 tsp (4 cl) oloroso sherry (you can also add up to 4 bsp/ 2 cl sugar syrup, depending how sweet the sherry is)
4 bsp (2 cl) cream
ground nutmeg for decorating

Thoroughly shake all the main ingredients in a shaker and filter into a cocktail glass; sprinkle with a little ground nutmeg.

Broker's Flip

3 tbsp (5 cl) white port
1 tbsp (1.5 cl) gin
2 bsp (1 cl) vermouth bianco
1 egg
1–2 dashes anisette
ground nutmeg for decorating

Thoroughly shake the main ingredients in a shaker and serve in a cocktail glass, sprinkled with ground nutmeg.

Chocolate Flip

3 tbsp (5 cl) port
1 bsp (0.5 cl) Chartreuse (yellow)
2 bsp (1 cl) white crème de cacao
1 egg
1 bsp (0.5 cl) sugar syrup
dark chocolate for grating

Thoroughly shake all the main ingredients in a shaker and filter into a cocktail glass. Sprinkle with a little grated dark chocolate.

Invigorating: eggnogs

An eggnog is equal to half a breakfast: egg yolk, sugar, cream, and one or more spirits. The Americans drink eggnogs at Christmas, for breakfast with a hangover, or for brunch, without alcohol if preferred. George Washington, the first president of the United States, was a declared fan and treated his guests to eggnogs made according to his own recipes. When making eggnogs, be sure to use the freshest eggs from a reliable source. Do not use raw egg yolk unless you are satisfied that it is safe.

Linguists have identified its origins in East Anglia, a rural area in the east of Eng-

Brandy and

Of all the spirits, those distilled from wine still enjoy a special cachet. Dutch seafarers and merchants were the ones who successfully distributed them in Europe and beyond. The rise of brandies became meteoric when two significant factors came into play: origin and aging. To this day, they determine the quality and the price.

In terms of volume, the global leader in brandy is McDowell No. 1, which is made in Bangalore, India. The Philippines appears right at the top of the list of confirmed brandy consumers, and in the USA more than one in three empty brandy bottles has been imported from the Cognac region. Although it is no exaggeration to describe brandy as one of the leading international drinks, its most famous and prestigious representatives continue to come from the countries that were most important in its history: France and Spain.

From the end of the 16th century, on account of their country's growth as a maritime and trading power, Dutch ships docked regularly in European ports. Among the goods traded

Chests destined for export are loaded onto a gabare (one of the standard cargo ships) in front of Hennessy's on the quayside in Cognac (ca. 1920).

land. The word *nog* is said to have derived from the 17th-century *noggin*, meaning a strong ale that was often mixed with egg. In Scotland old man's milk, as egg-nogs are called, is still served at Christmas and New Year. The Americans allege that the transformation of *egg* and *grog* — an earlier colloquial term for a mixture of rum, water, lemon juice, and sugar—into the commonly known *eggnog* is a genuine American invention. The eggnog has made its way round the world. It is drunk in the southern states of the USA with Bourbon, in Puerto Rico as *coquito*, as *rompope* in Mexico, and the French enjoy a *lait de poule*. It is modified slightly in every country. The Peruvians celebrate the start of the holidays with *biblia con pisco.*

cognac

were brandies, which promised ample profits and went on to establish a flourishing line of business—especially in the Jerez triangle, and in the Armagnac and Cognac regions—thanks to soaring demand. The third episode of the brandy story began in the 17th century, when it was noticed (presumably in many cellars about the same time) that storing the young, colorless distillate produced a completely transformed product: a milder brandy, gleaming gold with a fragrant scent of sweet spices, dried fruits, and smoky aromas. The first to catch on was cognac, or "coniack" brandy, followed by Armagnac, and then eventually Jerez brandy, trailing behind at the end of the 19th century.

While ordinary brandies play a leading role in the ensemble that goes to make up many trendy cocktails, topping the scale in terms of quality are the solo artists: cognacs, Armagnacs, and Solera Gran Reservas from Jerez help the connoisseur to find the most subtle sensory experiences at a sublime intellectual level.

Careful sampling of the cognacs, as seen here at Hennessy's in the 1930s, has always been a priority for cellar masters.

Invigorating: eggnogs

Brandy Eggnog

1 egg yolk
1 bsp (0.5 cl) sugar
1 oz (3 cl) brandy
1 tbsp (1.5 cl) white rum
3 tbsp (5 cl) cream
ground nutmeg and ground cinnamon, according to taste, for garnishing

Using a whisk, beat the egg yolk and sugar together in a shaker glass until the mixture turns pale. Add the brandy, rum, cream, and lots of ice to the shaker and shake thoroughly. Filter into a goblet containing a few ice cubes; sprinkle with ground nutmeg and ground cinnamon according to taste.

Breakfast Eggnog

1 egg yolk
2 oz (6 cl) brandy
1 tbsp (1.5 cl) orange curaçao
3 tbsp (5 cl) milk
3 tsp (4 cl) cream

Thoroughly shake all the ingredients in a shaker with ice. Filter into a large tumbler of crushed ice. This is a slightly milder but nevertheless well-flavored drink. Whether it is suitable for serving at breakfast, however, is a matter of personal opinion.

Advokaat's Eggnog

1 egg yolk
1 oz (3 cl) advocaat
2 oz (6 cl) tawny port
3 tsp (4 cl) milk
4 bsp (2 cl) cream
ground nutmeg for garnishing

Thoroughly shake all the main ingredients in a shaker with plenty of ice cubes, filter into a cocktail glass, and decorate with a little ground nutmeg.

A recipe from Charles Schumann's bar in Munich.

Mexican Eggnog

5 oz (15 cl) milk
1 oz (25 g) sugar
1 oz (25 g) ground almonds
1 egg yolk
3 tsp (4 cl) dark rum
4 bsp (2 cl) dark tequila
flaked almonds for garnishing

Bring the milk, sugar, and almonds to the boil and simmer for about 15 minutes, stirring all the time until you have a smooth liquid. Leave to cool and place in a shaker together with the egg yolk, rum, tequila, and plenty of ice. Shake well and filter into a chilled cocktail glass. Garnish with flaked almonds.

Invigorating: pick-me-ups

Pick-me-ups are intended to straighten up weary revelers with their throbbing heads and thick tongues the next morning. You are essentially on your own with your hangover as even scientists do not know for sure what happens in the head and what the best remedy for "alcoholic post intoxication syndrome" is. Up to now researchers have not considered it necessary to undertake a clinical investigation of one of the most frequent, albeit self-inflicted, of all headaches. The alcohol itself does not cause a hangover, however. It is the added ingredients. The key suspects include acetaldehyde—the very word grates on your nerves—and fusel oils, an unpopular side-product of distilling that is especially prevalent in brown distillates such as brandy and whiskey. These are then often combined with colorants and sulfur, which does not help the situation. Sticking to clear spirits in the event of above-average consumption in order to be on the safe side when it comes

Bitters without

The history of angostura bitters began in Venezuela, where the German doctor Johann Gottlieb Benjamin Siegert served the South American liberator Simon Bolivar during the wars of independence against the Spanish. Bolivar posted his army doctor as head of the field hospital in the Venezuelan town of Angostura (now Cuidad Bolivar). To alleviate the tropical diseases the soldiers were suffering from, Dr. Siegert searched for an antifebrile tonic. For four years he carried out research on tropical herbs, before being able to produce the curative Amargo Aromatico (aromatic bitters). The ingredients list includes angelica, cinchona, gentian, galangal, ginger, red sandalwood, and cinnamon, as well as cardamom, nutmeg, mace, cloves, bitter orange peel, and tonka beans. What is missing is angostura bark, which is part of the outer bark of a tree native to the Orinoco; the indigenous people were familiar with its antifebrile properties. The macerate is dark reddish-brown and very bitter.

Why Dr. Siegert's angostura gets by without angostura is unexplained, though this was immaterial to his fever-sick patients, whose numbers gradually went down. Word spread about the success, and the proximity of the trading port, Angostura, made such a radical difference to its export that the doctor exchanged his white coat for the to hangovers can backfire. As we know, however, to every rule there is an exception. As a chain-smoking cigar smoker, Winston Churchill used to consume large quantities of French cognac and remained free of hangovers. Yet one sip of the late Queen Mum's crystal clear gin and the prime minister looked miserable the next day. Low quality fruit brandies can also have disastrous consequences, even though they are transparent.

In addition to fusel oils, further suspects include the so-called congeners that are found more often in darker alcohols than in lighter ones and can cause nausea and headaches. The most malicious of all the added ingredients, however, is methanol or methylated spirit. In contrast to ethanol, the drinking alcohol, its toxic brother is broken down more slowly, forming formaldehyde and formic acid, which cause excruciating headaches and, in high doses, even blindness. Methanol therefore has its greatest effect on the body once the alcohol has been almost completely broken down. And this is where the body has its chance to outwit the alcohol. The breaking down of the ethanol is primarily the job of the liver, so if you start the next day with a Bloody Mary, your liver stops breaking down the methanol—according to the theory anyway—therefore stopping the hangover, temporarily. If you do not have any faith in this theory you can leave out the alcohol. Most of the remaining ingredients should help prevent hangovers. The best solution, however, is to exercise restraint before it gets to this stage.

angostura

overalls of a bitter liqueur manufacturer. Only then did he name his product for the town in which it originated. In 1875, when the political situation became more uncertain, the doctor emigrated to Trinidad with his sons and his company.

Their top seller soon became less important as a domestic remedy, but became a flavor enhancer instead. Not unknown in cookies, fruit salads, soups, sauces, and desserts, angostura bitters is most at home in the bar, where it forms part of the basic equipment. Many recipes testify to its versatility, but it is best known as a cleverly added dash to cocktails like the Mojito or the Manhattan.

Invigorating: pick-me-ups

Bloody Mary

3 tbsp (5 cl) vodka
5 oz (15 cl) tomato juice
1 dash lemon juice
1 dash Worcestershire sauce
1 dash Tabasco
black pepper
salt

Shake all the main ingredients well in a shaker and filter
into a large tall glass with two ice cubes.

Bull Shot

3 tbsp (5 cl) vodka
6 tbsp (10 cl) beef stock, preferably fresh but chilled

Combine the ingredients in a mixing glass. Season well.
Filter into a tall glass with ice cubes and stir. A strong
beef stock will help anyone in need of a little support to
get back on their feet.

Prairie Oyster

olive oil , 1–2 tbsp ketchup, 1 egg yolk
salt, freshly ground black pepper, 1 drop Tabasco
1 dash Worcestershire sauce
1–2 dashes balsamic vinegar or lemon juice
1 drop angostura and/or 2–4 bsp (1–2 cl) cognac

Wipe out a margarita glass with olive oil, place the ketchup in the glass, put the egg yolk on top, and season with
salt and freshly ground black pepper, Tabasco, Worcestershire sauce, and balsamic vinegar or lemon juice. You
can add angostura and/or cognac according to taste.

Fallen Angel

3 tsp (4 cl) gin
1 dash crème de menthe
1 dash angostura
1 dash lemon juice

Shake all the ingredients in a shaker with crushed ice and
filter into a cocktail glass. A Fallen Angel is the hair of
the dog that bit you for anyone that overindulged on gin
the night before. Tt is common knowledge that you can
cure like with like—or, according to the homeopathic
axiom, Similia similibus curantur.

Salubrious: after-dinner drinks

A good meal without a digestif used to be unthinkable. Nobody would have stood up from the table without ending the meal with a good cognac, a sweet cocktail, or a fine French liqueur. Each of these drinks has its own appeal after a generous meal. A cognac with coffee encourages relaxed contemplation. An ice-cold green Chartreuse helps to calm the stomach. A simple sweet and creamy cocktail can be far better than many a dessert. Many of these treats have unfortunately become forgotten. Well-intentioned but exaggerated healthy eating means that more and more delicious meals are served and concluded with water. Happily enough, however, the after-dinner drinks are still there, braving the storm, and they can also be drunk without a meal.

Liqueurs: medicinal purposes

Blossoms, berries, fruits, herbs and (depending on the plant) leaves, stems, roots, peels, barks or seeds, all make good ingredients in the production of liqueurs, which were pioneered by Arnaldus de Villanova. On his return from an Oriental crusade he brought with him the secrets of distillation, and used alcohol for medicinal purposes in the first half of the 13th century. Arnaldus macerated a wide range of medicinal plants in alcohol and rounded off the flavor with honey.

For many years, these elixirs were mainly used as remedies and tonics by monks and apothecaries. As early as the 14th century, recipes began to appear which put greater

The Chartreuse monastery in the French Alps

POUSSE-CAFÉS

Pousse-cafés are also known as rainbow drinks or scaffas and are labor intensive because they require a very complicated technique, but the optical effect is unbeatable. The ingredients must be of different colors and must not mix with one another when poured into the glass, instead remaining visible as clear layers one on top of the other. This is achieved using the physical densities of the ingredients. You start with a sugary syrup, and each of the following layers must contain less sugar but more alcohol than the layer beneath it. Most bartenders pour the ingredients carefully over the back of a bar spoon into the glass. Or, even better, you can pour the ingredients into the glass via a thin spout at one end of a bar spoon that has the spoon at the other end.

The quantities are measured so that equal or almost equal layers are created in either ascending or descending order. Ideally, you finish with a high-proof spirit but, in case that is too strong to be served to your guests as a drink, you can instead serve a pousse-café aflame: that gets rid of some of the alcohol and you create a spectacular effect with it.

and enjoyment

emphasis on the enjoyment factor. This in turn led to the emergence of actual liqueurs, and the availability of canesugar and spices from faraway countries made it possible to refine them. Prospects for liqueur producers only improved at the end of the 19th century, due to the passion for all things Oriental at that time. This exoticism was epitomized by sweet oranges and Dutch Curaçao, which was made from bitter oranges. However, this product was dark, heavy and excessively aromatic, so Edouard Cointreau devised a simple, crystal clear version. This marked the decisive breakthrough for liqueurs, as well as the establishment of the great brand names globally.

The elegant world on the advertising poster for Bénédictine

Salubrious: after-dinner drinks

BBC

3 tsp (4 cl) brandy
4 bsp (2 cl) Bénédictine
3 tsp (4 cl) cream

Thoroughly shake the ingredients in a shaker and filter into a tumbler with ice cubes.

Despite its name, the drink is not particularly newsworthy. The name is merely based on the combination of brandy, Bénédictine, and cream.

Alaska

3 tsp (4 cl) gin
4 bsp (2 cl) Chartreuse
few dashes bitter orange

Stir the ingredients together well in a mixing glass and filter into a small goblet. An Alaska is a good example of the almost forgotten positive effect of liqueurs after a meal.

Angel's Delight

4 bsp (2 cl) gin
4 bsp (2 cl) Grand Marnier
2 dashes grenadine
3 tsp (4 cl) cream

Shake all the ingredients together well in a shaker and then pour into a cocktail glass. The color is enough to delight any angel.

Brandy Alexander

1 oz (3 cl) cognac
4 bsp (2 cl) crème de cacao
1 oz (3 cl) cream
ground nutmeg for decorating

Thoroughly shake the main ingredients in a shaker. Filter into a cocktail glass and sprinkle with ground nutmeg.

Brandy Alexander is a classic with some high-profile relatives such as the Alexander, Alexandra (with gin and cream), and Alexander's Sister (with crème de menthe instead of crème de cacao).

Salubrious: sweet drinks

Beach at Night

3 tsp (4 cl) rum
2 bsp (1 cl) almond syrup
3 tsp (4 cl) orange juice
4 bsp (2 cl) lemon juice
2 oz (6 cl) mango juice
4 bsp (2 cl) cream
4 bsp (2 cl) blue curaçao
star fruit and lemon peel for garnishing

Shake all the ingredients except the last two in a shaker
with ice. Filter into a tall glass with ice cubes, add the
blue curaçao, and garnish with star fruit and lemon peel.

El Presidente

3 tsp (4 cl) white rum
2 bsp (1 cl) triple sec
2 bsp (1 cl) dry vermouth
2 bsp (1 cl) grenadine
2 bsp (1 cl) lime juice

Stir all the ingredients in a mixing glass with ice cubes
and filter into a chilled cocktail glass.

El Presidente is a Cuban classic and needs no garnishing
at all.

Nine Mile

3 tbsp (5 cl) dark rum
4 bsp (2 cl) banana liqueur
2 bsp (1 cl) vanilla syrup
2 bsp (1 cl) cassis
2 bsp (1 cl) lime juice
2½ oz (7 cl) pineapple juice
2 oz (6 cl) cranberry juice
fruit for garnishing

Shake all the main ingredients together well in a shaker and filter into a tall glass filled half full with crushed ice. Garnish with fruit.

Midnight Moon

2 bsp (1 cl) cognac
2 bsp (1 cl) amaretto
2 bsp (1 cl) Cacao Pico
champagne

Stir the first three ingredients together in an ice-cold mixing glass with ice cubes. Filter into a chilled cocktail glass and top up with ice-cold champagne.

Another cocktail that needs no garnishing.

Salubrious: cold coffee drinks

Blackjack

2 bsp (1 cl) brandy
1 oz (3 cl) kirsch
1 oz (3 cl) cold espresso
4 bsp (2 cl) sugar syrup

Shake all the ingredients in a shaker with ice. Filter into a cocktail glass with crushed ice and serve with a straw.

Black Prince

4 bsp (2 cl) white rum
2 bsp (1 cl) coconut syrup
1 oz (3 cl) cream
2 oz (6 cl) cold espresso
1 tbsp (1.5 cl) orgeat (almond syrup)
dark chocolate for garnishing

Shake all the main ingredients together well in a shaker
with ice. Filter into a chilled goblet with shaved ice.
Sprinkle with grated dark chocolate.

Kahlúa Frappé

4 bsp (2 cl) Kahlúa
4 bsp (2 cl) white crème de cacao
2 bsp (1 cl) amaretto
4 bsp (2 cl) coconut syrup
lightly whipped cream
cocoa powder for garnishing

Shake the first four ingredients together well in a shaker.
Filter into a tall goblet with shaved ice. Top up with about
half to 1 inch (2 cm) lightly whipped cream and serve
sprinkled with cocoa.

Cappuccino Freddo

3 oz (8 cl) cold espresso
1 oz (3 cl) Kahlúa
1 oz (3 cl) brandy
warm milk
cocoa powder and ground cinnamon for garnishing

Combine the first three ingredients in a glass with shaved
ice and stir. Whip some warm milk and pour into the
glass; sprinkle with cocoa powder and ground cinnamon.

Salubrious: pousse-cafés

Flatliner

Sambuca
Tabasco
Tequila

Not a drink for gentle souls. It does have some appeal as a strong digestif, however. ▼

Rainbow Warrior

Grenadine
Blue curaçao
Crème de banane
Maraschino
Chartreuse (yellow)
brandy

◄

A drink for gallant warriors. The individual layers can be sucked up with a silver straw. At least that way you know what you are in for.

4th of July

Grenadine
Blue curaçao
Batida de Côco

This is likely to please every American. Whether it also tastes good is another question.

B-52

Tia Maria
Baileys
Grand Marnier

The B-52 is one of the few pousse-cafés that is ordered relatively often. Connoisseurs order a Bifi.

Heated: hot punches, slings, and toddies

Heating alcohol is a delicate matter. It starts to evaporate at around 158 °F (70 °C) and anyone that allows a saucepan of Glühwein to boil away will be left with nothing more than an insipid, sticky, sweet mixture. On the other hand, warm alcohol enters the bloodstream more quickly, as will be confirmed by anyone who drinks a hot punch after skiing or warms their frozen soul with a hot grog at the water's edge.

Hot punches are not only known in cold regions, even though they are usually drunk in winter and, of course, every country has their own punch. Ever since chilly carol singers were welcomed into English country houses with their halls decked with holly and mistletoe, flaming punch has become a part of Christmas tradition. In contrast to their chilled, summery white wine relatives, hot punches are made with red wine spiced with the likes of cloves, cinnamon, and lemon and

Dark rum:

A tried and trusted method of aging rum is in used Bourbon barrels. Maturing in wood intensifies the color of the rum, giving it first a light gold tone, then amber or mahogany tones that some cellarers will assist by adding caramel. One peculiarity of the maturing of rum in the West Indies consists in the effects of the hot tropical climate. Anyone entering a warehouse full of barrels will be overwhelmed by the intensive odor. The proportion of distillate evaporating at high temperatures is considered to be 7–8% per year.

Contemporary representations of sugarcane harvesting and processing in Cuba during the 19th century

orange peel and heated. A cozy winter atmosphere develops as soon as the sugar is melted by the heat.

The world's largest bowl of flaming punch was prepared at Munich's Isartor in December 2005, when 2,380 gallons (9,000 liters) of punch were heated in a 10-foot (3 m) high copper kettle with a diameter of 8 feet (2.5 m). Of course, you can get away with making a smaller punch for what you need at home. However, the favorite recipes are almost always made for the whole family because they are best enjoyed in company. The quantities given here are sufficient for about six people. The other recipes are for four generous servings.

SLINGS AND TODDIES

A toddy is traditionally a kind of grog, heated alcohol with spices and hot water, often also with tea. Due to its climatic conditions Scotland is considered to be the home of the hot toddy. Slings have similar basic ingredients but were first mixed on the other side of the Atlantic.

Today even cold drinks with the same basic ingredients are also referred to as a sling or a toddy, but the old recipes still have their appeal. In principle, a base spirit is combined with a hot liquid such as tea and an aromatic ingredient. Honey or cane-sugar syrup provides the sweetness.

growing old in the tropics

With accelerated aging, rum can be classified as mature after just three years. It will then, depending on whether new or older barrels were used, have a more or less intensely spicy or roasted note. However, to be able to develop multilayered aromas blending notes of tropical fruits, spices, cocoa, and tobacco, rum requires a significantly longer maturation period. It will reach the next stage after 6 to 8 years, while the most outstanding rums are left to mature for longer than 10, 15, or 20 years.

Rum is usually aged in small Bourbon barrels or in large vats for quicker maturation.

Heated: hot punches

Feuerzangenbowle

zest of 1 organic orange
zest of 1 organic lemon
juice of the organic orange
1 dash lemon juice
50 oz (150 cl) red wine
6 tbsp (10 cl) orange juice
1 cinnamon stick
2 cloves
sugar loaf
dark rum (at least 54% vol.)
½ vanilla pod and star anise (optional)

Zest the orange and lemon thinly so that none of the white pith adheres to the zest. Then squeeze the citrus fruit, and slowly heat the juice of the orange and a dash of the lemon juice with the red wine and the 6 tbsp (10 cl) of orange juice. Add the zest to the saucepan. Flavor with the cinnamon stick, cloves, and (according to taste) the halved vanilla pod and the star anise. Warm the mixture only—do not boil. Leave to infuse on the stove for a good 15 minutes. Shortly before serving pour into a fireproof bowl on a burner. Some specialist bowls have a perforated surface for the sugar loaf. Otherwise use a long pair of tongs. The sugar loaf is soaked in a small ladle of dark rum and then set alight. The heat melts and caramelizes the sugar so that it drips into the bowl, forming little floating islands of fire. The Feuerzangenbowle is then ready.

Jean Gabin

8 oz (24 cl) dark rum
4 oz (12 cl) Calvados
6 tbsp (10 cl) maple syrup
milk
ground nutmeg and a piece of apple for garnishing

Place the rum, Calvados, and maple syrup in a saucepan and make up to 2 pints (1 liter) with milk before heating. Serve in fire-proof glasses sprinkled with ground nutmeg.

Rum Orange Punch

5 oz (16 cl) orange juice
3 tsp (4 cl) Southern Comfort
7 oz (20 cl) dark rum
3 oz (8 cl) lemon juice
3 oz (8 cl) lime juice
4 bsp (2 cl) sugar syrup
zest of 1 lemon (organic)
zest of 1 orange (organic)

Place the first six ingredients in a saucepan and heat without allowing to boil. Pour into fire-proof glasses, sprinkle with the citrus zest, and serve.

Amsterdam Punch

5 oz (16 cl) dark rum
27 oz (80 cl) black tea
4 bsp (2 cl) sugar syrup
1 pinch ground nutmeg
1 pinch cinnamon, 1 clove

Gently heat all the main ingredients, leave to infuse, and pour into fire-proof glasses.

Heated: slings and toddies

Apple Toddy

1 bsp (0.5 cl) canesugar syrup
3 tbsp (5 cl) Calvados
warm cider

Combine the canesugar syrup and Calvados, and then top up with warm cider.

Hot Dram

3 tbsp (5 cl) Drambuie
1 tbsp (1.5 cl) lemon juice
a few dashes orange juice , cinnamon stick for stirring

Combine the Drambuie and lemon juice in a fire-proof glass and add a few dashes of orange juice. Top up with hot water and stir with a cinnamon stick.

Hot Toddy

1 tbsp honey
4 bsp (2 cl) lemon juice
1 oz (3 cl) whiskey

Combine the honey and lemon juice in a fire-proof glass beaker, top up with hot water, and stir before adding the whiskey.

Vodka Sling

2 oz (6 cl) vodka
2 bsp forest honey
4 bsp (2 cl) orange juice

Combine all the ingredients and top up with hot water.

Heated: hot coffee drinks

Irish Coffee

1 double espresso (approx.
2½ oz / 7 cl strong black coffee)
1 oz (3 cl) Irish whiskey
2 bsp sugar
lightly whipped cream

Place a spoon in an Irish Coffee glass so that the glass doesn't crack. Combine the first three ingredients in the glass and stir. Carefully fill the top quarter of the glass with whipped cream up to the rim. The more sugar there is dissolved in the coffee, the easier it is. It should look like a freshly poured Guinness.

Russian Nuts

1 tbsp (1.5 cl) vodka
4 bsp (2 cl) Kahlúa
2 bsp (1 cl) macadamia syrup
1 double espresso , lightly whipped cream

Combine the first three ingredients and heat. Place a bar spoon in a liqueur glass to prevent it cracking. Pour in the mixture, add the double espresso, stir, and top up to the rim with the lightly whipped cream.

Banana Coffee

4 bsp (2 cl) cognac
4 bsp (2 cl) Baileys
2 bsp (1 cl) Kahlúa
2 bsp (1 cl) crème de banane
1 espresso, 1 pinch cinnamon for garnishing

Combine all the main ingredients and garnish with a pinch of cinnamon. It is important that all the liquids are hot.

IRISH WHISKEY

Considered the whiskey par excellence during the 19th century, "pure pot still" from Ireland had to be more or less reinvented after World War II. Irish whiskey is now typically smooth and light, with floral notes and a hint of citrus fruit that give way to vanilla, dried fruit, and nuts, producing an especially well-balanced flavor. This profile has guaranteed it a place alongside Scotch and Bourbon. While this is mainly down to Irish Distillers, with its portfolio of triple-distilled famous brands, Cooley has revived the Irish pot still with great results.

Virgin (non-alcoholic) drinks

SHERBETS AND FREEZES

Alcohol, its abuse, its mind-enhancing effects, and its influence on social connections are a significant component of bar history. However, there have also always been guests who, for different reasons, do not drink alcohol. Instead of ordering water and fruit juice they wanted accomplished drinks without alcohol and they got them. Many of these drinks compensate for the lack of alcohol with elaborate ingredients and garnishes. Sherbets usually feature a floating ball of half-frozen sorbet. Sodas shine with exotic ingredients such as ginger and basil, while cream and ice cream spruce up mixed milk drinks.

Legend has it that the upper classes of ancient Greece and Rome had discovered ice for their revelries in order to chill their wine and honey mixture. Runners collected the snow from the mountains by working in relays with the filled containers.

There are also reports of early ice consumption in China, and later in France as well. Catherine de Medici, born in Tuscany, is said to have brought ice cream recipes from her homeland with her to Paris, as well as a number of other things that also influenced French cuisine. The recipes spread from there to western Europe. Icy concoctions with rose petals, cherries, and a variety of spices had long been bestsellers in Turkey. The belief in the healthy proper-

ties of sorbets was common in the gardens of the Ottoman empire, where apothecaries and physicians monitored the quality of the plants and where a sherbet is still served at childbirth today, being considered an aid to stimulating milk production.

At the bar sherbets are drinks made partly of sorbet. Either the sorbet can be bought readymade or you can go to the trouble of making it yourself—which will probably result in a much more sophisticated version.

MOCKTAILS

Mocktails, a combination of the words "cocktail" and "mock," have become a standard bar feature despite their disparaging name. Initially they were existing drinks with the alcoholic components left out and cleverly replaced with other flavorings. False cocktails have long been a species in their own right, with their own competitions being staged among bartenders. The latter do not have to be asked twice and come up with one exotic creation after the other. Alcohol-free drinks have become a very dynamic category among bar drinks. And for those who do not want to go completely without, there are always the mocktails with a dash of something extra. Not really an alcoholic drink, but not a party pooper either.

Raspberry Grape Sherbet

2½ oz (7 cl) white grape juice
2 bsp (1 cl) sugar syrup
1 dash lime juice, 1 scoop raspberry sorbet
Indian tonic, 1 strip lemon peel for garnishing

Shake the first three ingredients well in a shaker. Filter into a large cocktail glass and add a scoop of raspberry sorbet. Top up with Indian tonic and garnish with a strip of lemon peel.

Coco Yogurt Sherbet

4 oz (12 cl) organic yogurt
3 tbsp (5 cl) coconut cream
1 oz (3 cl) acacia honey
2 bsp (1 cl) vanilla syrup
1 scoop blue curaçao sorbet

Puree the first six ingredients in an electric mixer. Place the redcurrant liqueur in a large goblet. Add the mixture from the mixer, stirring briefly so that both liquids are mixed together slightly. Garnish with fresh raspberries.

Strawberry Choc Freeze

1 oz (3 cl) strawberry syrup
4 bsp (2 cl) chocolate syrup
2 oz (6 cl) cranberry juice
1 bsp raspberry jam
grated dark chocolate and fruit for garnishing

Mix all the main ingredients with lots of crushed ice in an electric mixer. The mixture should be cold and thick but not so thick that a spoon can stand up in it. Garnish with grated dark chocolate and fruit on the rim of the glass.

Virgin: mocktails

Hurricane Mocktail

2 oz (6 cl) orange juice
2 oz (6 cl) cranberry juice
1 oz (3 cl) grapefruit juice
1 oz (3 cl) apple juice
kumquat, lime, and star fruit for garnishing

Shake all the main ingredients together well in a shaker.
Filter into a hurricane glass with crushed ice, garnish with
a kumquat, a piece of lime, and a slice of star fruit, and
serve with a straw.

Mai Tai Mocktail

4 bsp (2 cl) orange juice
4 bsp (2 cl) almond syrup
4 bsp (2 cl) lime cordial
2 bsp (1 cl) lime juice
2 bsp (1 cl) canesugar syrup
3 drops angostura
lime slice for garnishing

Shake all the main ingredients together in a shaker. Filter
into a large cocktail glass of crushed ice, garnish the rim
with a slice of lime, and serve with a straw.

Champagne Faux

6 tbsp (10 cl) white grape juice
2 bsp (1 cl) chaï syrup (green tea concentrate)
tonic
grape slices for garnishing

Combine the grape juice and chaï syrup and shake well.
Filter into a champagne flute, top up with tonic, and garnish with paper-thin grape slices.

Shirley Temple

1 oz (3 cl) grenadine
2 oz (6 cl) orange juice
ginger ale or another soda
star fruit, orange, and kiwi fruit (for example) for
garnishing

Place the grenadine in a large goblet and fill with crushed
ice. Carefully add the orange juice and top up with ginger
ale or another soda. Garnish generously with fruit.

Originally a drink served to children so that they could
take part in celebratory toasts, this has since become a
standard feature in any classic bar.

Virgin: exotic lemonades

Ginger & Mint Lemonade

3 thin slices of fresh ginger
1 sprig of mint
1 oz (3 cl) lemon juice
4 bsp (2 cl) canesugar syrup
4 oz (12 cl) soda water
1 sprig mint for garnishing

Place the fresh ginger and the leaves from a sprig of mint in an Old Fashioned glass. Crush gently with a pestle. Shake the lemon juice and canesugar syrup together in a shaker and filter into the glass with ice cubes. Top up with soda water and place a sprig of mint in the glass.

Cranberry Lemonade

1 oz (3 cl) lemon juice
4 bsp (2 cl) canesugar syrup
3 tsp (4 cl) cranberry juice
6 tbsp (10 cl) soda water
lemon and strawberry for garnishing

Shake the first three ingredients together in a shaker. Filter into an Old Fashioned glass with ice cubes. Top up with soda water and garnish with a piece of lemon and strawberry.

Basil and Grape Lemonade

Basil leaves
1 oz (3 cl) lemon juice
4 bsp (2 cl) canesugar
3 tsp (4 cl) white grape juice
3 red grapes
4 oz (12 cl) soda water
2 basil leaves for garnishing

Place the first three ingredients in a large Old Fashioned glass and crush gently with a pestle. Add the white grape juice together with the red grapes and an ice cube. Top up with soda water. Stir briefly and garnish with basil leaves. Serve with a straw.

Grapefruit Lemonade

1 oz (3 cl) lemon juice
4 bsp (2 cl) cane-sugar syrup
3 tsp (4 cl) pink grapefruit juice
4 oz (12 cl) soda water
1 piece grapefruit peel for garnishing.

Virgin: smoothies

Blackcurrant Smoothie

2 tbsp pineapple puree
2 tbsp passion fruit puree
2 bsp (1 cl) sugar syrup
4 bsp (2 cl) pineapple juice
3 tbsp blackcurrants
2 bsp (1 cl) sugar syrup
1 oz (3 cl) creamy yogurt
1 bsp passion fruit puree
fruit pieces for garnishing

Shake the first four ingredients together in a shaker and place in a hurricane glass. Shake the blackcurrants with the sugar syrup in a shaker. Pour the creamy yogurt into the pineapple—passion fruit mixture and then add the blackcurrant puree. Stir the liquids a little so that the colors run, and then top with passion fruit puree. Garnish with pieces of fruit.

The intensive flavor and the velvety consistency of pureed fruit in a smoothie are hard to beat. The pureed fruit is of course the most important ingredient. You can be sure that smoothies bought at the supermarket contain more than just fruit. Many of the commercially produced "all fruit" smoothies contain sugar (some of them have even more sugar than cola), are expensive, and are pasteurized, but—because of their fiber content—are still better than most fruit juices. Just not as good as homemade.

Pureeing fruit is not difficult—you simply remove everything that is not meant to end up in the glass, such as pits. The skin is peeled or else the fruit is dipped briefly into boiling water and the skin then removed. Fruit needing hardly any cleaning, such as strawberries or raspberries, can be used deep frozen. That means you don't need the cubes when mixing. The fruit then has to be pureed in an electric mixer. This normally requires a certain amount of liquid, preferably a bought fruit juice from the same fruit or another liquid component of the drink-to-be. Any skin or pit residues can be filtered out at this stage.

Almost any kind of fruit can be mixed with another sort. Three almost always work, but with more fruit the flavor becomes somewhat uniform. Suitable ingredients include milk, creamy yogurt, and ice cream, as well as boosters such as soy milk and green tea. The individual quantities do not have to be strictly adhered to. What is important is that the finished drink feels soft and creamy—smooth—to the tongue.

Kiwi Cranberry Smoothie

2 peeled kiwi fruit
4 bsp (2 cl) milk
4 bsp (2 cl) cream
2 bsp acacia honey
approx. 3 tbsp cranberries
cranberry juice
kiwi fruit and Cape gooseberries for garnishing

Place the first five ingredients in an electric mixer and puree them. While the motor is still running, add cranberry juice through the opening in the top until the drink has a smooth consistency. Add some crushed ice to chill the drink.

Mango Smoothie

½ mango, peeled, flesh removed from the pit
4 yellow plums, ripe, peeled, pits removed
6 strawberries
3 tsp (4 cl) cream
3 tbsp yogurt
3 tsp (4 cl) green tea
passion fruit juice
fruit wedge and 1 sprig mint for garnishing

Cut the mango into pieces against the grain of the flesh, otherwise the long fibers will jam the mixer. Place in a mixer together with the plums, strawberries, cream, yogurt, and green tea, adding some passion fruit juice if necessary to reach the right consistency. Add some crushed ice. Leave the mixer running until everything is thoroughly mixed. Serve in a brandy balloon garnished with a wedge of fruit and a sprig of mint.

Virgin: mixed milk drinks

Vanilla Passion

....

5 oz (150 g) yogurt
4 bsp (2 cl) vanilla syrup
4 bsp (2 cl) lemon juice
2 oz (6 cl) passion fruit juice
mint and a piece vanilla pod for garnishing

Mix all the main ingredients with some crushed ice in an
electric mixer. Fill a fancy glass with 1 bar scoop full of
crushed ice and pour in the mixture. Garnish with mint
and a piece of vanilla pod.

Yogurt makes up the milk component in many
milkshakes. It contains little fat but is still creamy. It all
depends on the quality: a cheap version from a discount
supermarket will always have the corresponding taste.

Strawberry Dream

....

5 oz (150 g) yogurt
4 bsp (2 cl) strawberry syrup
4 bsp (2 cl) lemon juice
2 oz (6 cl) passion fruit juice
strawberries and mint for garnishing

Mix all the main ingredients together in an electric mixer
with some crushed ice. Fill a fancy glass with crushed ice
and add the liquid. Garnish with strawberries and mint,
not forgetting a straw.

Pink Peach Smoothie

3 oz (8 cl) white peach puree
5 oz (150 g) yogurt
1 tbsp white cane sugar
1 bsp lemon juice
1 cocktail cherry for garnishing

Mix all the main ingredients in an electric mixer until you have a smooth mixture (the sugar needs to dissolve). Add some crushed ice through the opening in the top and leave the motor running until the drink is chilled. Place in an Old Fashioned glass, garnish with a cocktail cherry, and serve with a straw.

Virgin Swimming Pool

3 tbsp (5 cl) coconut cream
6 tbsp (10 cl) pineapple juice
1 bsp blue curaçao syrup
pineapple for garnishing

Mix all the main ingredients together in an electric mixer with crushed ice until the mixture is smooth. Pour into a fancy glass, garnish with pineapple, and serve with a straw.

Glossary

A

alembic   Arabic word for pot still adopted into many other languages.

A.O.C.   Appellation d'Origine Contrôlée; designation of origin of French wines and spirits, etc.

aperitif   Stimulating drink before meals; also the term used for the occasion (before lunch or dinner).

assemblage   Blending; mixing together the contents of different tanks or casks.

B

bonded distillery   Commercial distillery in which the alcohol produced is subject to spirits tax; the distilling equipment is therefore sealed by customs.

Boston shaker   Two part shaker made of a stirring glass and a steel beaker; a separate sieve is used for straining.

botanicals   Plants and parts of plants from which aromas and flavors are extracted.

built in glass   Drink mixed in the glass in which it is served.

C

cask aging   Aging of wines and brandies in wood casks, mainly made of oak, in the course of which flavors are transferred to the distillate and alcohol evaporates.

centiliter (cl)   One hundredth of a liter; standard measure for cocktail ingredients, unless measured in fluid ounces (1 cl = 0.34 fl oz).

chai   Term used in southwest France for an above ground maturation cellar.

charge   Filling the pot still with one batch.

chill filtering   Type of cold filtering process used for most whiskies that clarifies but also reduces the flavors; whisk(e)y with an alcohol content of 46% vol. and above is not usually chill filtered.

chip ice   Ice broken into pieces smaller than an ice cube.

cocktail   Small mixed drink which (nearly always) contains strong alcoholic ingredients and is served in a goblet-shape glass.

Coffey still   Column still used for continuous distillation; perfected by Irishman Aeneas Coffey (1780–1852).

cold stabilization   Chilling wines and spirits to below freezing in order to remove particles and prevent clouding; reduces the flavor intensity.

column still   Distillation equipment in which distilling takes place without interruption (continuous process); as opposed to batch distillation in which the alcohol is concentrated during sequential passes.

cooling coil   Component of distilling equipment; alcohol vapors are passed through it and condensed by cold liquid.

crushed ice   Ice broken down into small pieces.

curaçao   Liqueur the blue colored version of which has become famous, made with bitter oranges from the eponymous island in the Dutch Antilles.

D

decanting   Pouring contents of a bottle into a carafe; essential in the case of vintage port, which develops a lot of sediment.

dephlegmator   Attachment to column still; provides added concentration.

digestif   Spirits, often made with herbal extracts, designed to aid digestion.

distillate High percentage product of distillation.

double chauffe Fr.: double distilled.

drinking strength Alcohol content of spirits reaching the market; fine spirit or spirits that have been cask aged contain too much alcohol and have to be broken down with water or *petites eaux*; hurrying the process leads to cloudiness.

E

eau-de-vie Fr.: water of life, spirit, distillate.

eggnog Type of punch made with eggs, also with cream.

elaboration Aging, maturation, of wines and spirits.

ethanol Scientific term for alcohol used in drinks.

etheric (or essential) oils Extracts from plants, or parts of plants, that have a distinctive aroma.

F

fillers Fruit juices and sodas that often form the largest part of mixed drinks.

fine spirit Second distillation, from which the distillate proper is obtained from the raw spirit.

flavoring parts Ingredients in mixed drinks that influence the taste of the final product significantly; e.g. angostura bitters, grenadine.

flip Mixed drink made with egg; the best known are eggnogs.

fluid ounce (fl oz) Measure for cocktail ingredients in many English-speaking countries; divided into units such as ½ fl. oz, ¾ fl. oz; 1 fl. oz = 2.93 cl.

fruit brandy, fruit "wasser" (e.g. kirschwasser) Distillate obtained from fermented fruits as indicated on the label.

fruit juice concentrate Fruit juice reduced in volume by steam extraction.

fruit juice drink Fruit component is 6–30% (depending on fruit type).

fruit nectar Fruit component is 25–50%.

fruit spirit, eau-de-vie Distillate of fruits macerated in neutral alcohol.

fusel oils By-products of fermentation, substances that may or may not be desirable, e.g. glycerine, succinic acid, higher alcohols; they are separated off in the heads and tails. Palatable fusel oils can be added by distillers to give character to a spirit.

H

heads Condensation of easily volatile substances during distillation pass; contains undesirable substances and is separated off.

heart The middle part of the distillation pass, which is collected separately from the heads and tails (têtes and seconds).

highball Long drink made with a base spirit, juice, or soda and often a third ingredient; one of the oldest types of drink.

I

invert sugar Syrup made from sugar, water, and an acidic component (e.g. citric or ascorbic acid). When the mixture is heated the acid causes the sugar (sucrose) to break down into simple sugar, which does not crystallize as readily when cooled down. The syrup can therefore be far sweeter and yet remain liquid.

J

jigge Small beaker with calibrated measures used to measure liquids for cocktails. Calculated in fluid ounces in the English-speaking world, and by centiliter in continental Europe.

L

liqueur   Spirit with minimum of 15% vol. alcohol and minimum sugar content of 15 oz per gallon/ 100 g per liter (12 oz / 80 g for gentian liqueur; 11 oz / 70 g for cherry liqueur).

M

maceration   Steeping fruits in alcohol or wine to release their flavors and aromas.

malt   Grain brought to germination, mostly barley, the special enzymes of which can be used to convert the starch in the grain into sugar, a prerequisite for fermentation.

maraschino, maraschino cherry   Cherry liqueur from north Italy, ingredient in recipes (Singapore Sling, Sidecar); also very sweet candied cherries.

marc   Fr.: pomace.

martini glass   Classic cocktail glass with long stem and flat goblet shape; often used for martini cocktails.

mash   Lightly crushed fruits fermented with the must.

methanol   Alcohol not desirable in spirits as its metabolic products—formaldehyde and formic acid—are toxic.

minimum alcohol content   Alcohol content laid down by law for any traded spirit; also a criterion in spirit regulations used in defining specific types of spirit.

mise-en-place   Work preparation for bartenders and chefs: everything must be in the correct position within reach.

mistelle   Grape must in which fermentation is halted with alcohol; used as ingredient or sold as liqueur wine.

modifier   Ingredient in mixed drinks that alters the taste of the base spirit; classic example: vermouth in martini.

mutage   Fr. "silencing," also fortifying; stopping fermentation of alcohol by adding neutral alcohol or spirit; the yeasts responsible for fermentation die when the mash has an alcohol content of 17.5% vol.

N

neutral alcohol   Ethyl alcohol of agricultural origin, with no discernible taste, and a minimum alcohol content of 96% vol.

O

Old fashioned glass   Large, wide rimmed tumbler.

orgeat   Syrup made from almonds and other ingredients.

P

percentage volume (% vol.)   One hundredth unit of volume measurement.

percolation (Lat. percolare = to sieve through)   Method of extraction for plant substances.

petites eaux   Mixture of distilled water and cognac, armagnac, or other spirit; used to adjust the alcohol content to drinking strength.

plates   Component of distilling equipment: horizontal punched tray in a column still; the holes are extended upward with pipes that have bell-shape caps. The plates provide a larger contact surface for the gas mixture and liquid during the continuous process.

pomace   Solids remaining after the grapes have been pressed; also known as marc.

pot still   Traditional alembic still used for batch distillation—that is, sequential distilling (fractional process).

Prohibition   Ban on sales, production, and transport of alcohol in the USA, law passed on January 29,

1919, came into force on January 1, 1920; repealed on December 5, 1933.

R

raw spirit   Product of the first distillation run, which contains all the alcohol and most of the volatile substances. The weak distillate is concentrated into fine spirit, and unwanted components (fusel oils) are separated in the heads and tails.

rectification   Making alcohol more neutral tasting, and giving it a higher alcohol percentage, through repeated distillation.

residual sugar   Sugar not converted to alcohol during fermentation, giving a wine its natural sweetness.

S

snifter   Ideal glass for whisky and other cask aged spirits.

spent mash   Residue of fermented mash after distillation

spirits regulation   EU regulation NL 110/2008 of the European Parliament and Council of January 15, 2008, covering the definitions, descriptions, presentation, and labeling of spirits, as well as protecting the geographic details for spirits and replacing EU regulation NL 1576/89; published in European Union gazette of February 2, 2008.

still   Part of the distillery's equipment, used to heat mash or wines; now the established term for traditional equipment used for batch distillation.

sugar syrup   Syrup made by heating sugar and water (invert sugar).

swan's neck   Component of distilling equipment; copper pipe through which the rising alcohol vapors are led from the still to the condensing coil, or condenser.

T

tails   Last part of the distillation pass, in which non-volatile, undesirable, and partially harmful substances condense and are separated off.

triple sec   Colorless orange liqueur with alcohol content of over 25% vol.

tumbler   Small cylindrical glass traditionally used for whisk(e)y neat or on ice, also suitable for short drinks with ice.

V

V.S. Very Special   Term used to describe cognac aged for at least 2 years.

V.S.O.P. Very Superior Old Pale   Term used to describe spirits, especially cognac, aged at least 4 years.

W

wash   "Beer" with 7–9% alcohol by volume, initial substance used in whisky production.

wash back   Fermentation tank for whisky production.

wash still   Distillation equipment for the first distillation run for malt whisky.

wine prewarmer   Additional tank in distillation equipment, in which wine is used as a coolant for the spirit and is itself warmed up in the process before it flows into the still; reduces energy consumption of the plant.

wine spirit   Specialist term for fermented, fortified wine that is distilled to produce (bulk) brandies.

Index of cocktails

Index

Acknowledgements

Many individuals, companies and institutions helped in the production of this book. We would like to extend our sincere thanks to them. Unfortunately we cannot mention everyone, but we have tried to name – in the order they appear in the book – those who provided us with information and images. Our special thanks go to:

Green Door Cocktailbar Berlin, Winterfeldstr. 50, 10718 Berlin, www.greendoor.de;

Wilhelm-Fabry-Museum, Hilden;

Markus Holstein, Innovative Destillations-technik, Markdorf, www.a-holstein.de;

Cantine Florio Marsala;

Laurine Caute, BNIC, Cognac;

Roberto Ayala for the architects Emmanuel Picault and Ludwig Godefroy and the M-N. Roy in Mexico City;

Anna-Karin Olofsson, Peter F. Heering, Stockholm;

Christina Norton, Claridge's, The Connaught, The Berkeley, London;

Danielle Makhoul, DW5/ Bernard Khoury, Beirut;

Colleen Kong, 3GATTI Architecture Studio, Rome and Shanghai;

Ainslie Cheung, The Ritz-Carlton Hotel Company, Hong Kong;

Damion Lepp, Icebar by Icehotel, London;

Brian Gore, Bulgari Hotel & Residences London, 171 Knightsbridge, London;

Sonali Mukerjee and Maude Michel, Becca PR, New York for The Cosmopolitan of Las Vegas;

Philippe Starck and Mahaut Champetier de Ribes, Starck, Paris;

Dr. Tina Ingwersen-Matthiesen, Borco-Marken-Import, Hamburg;

Steffen Hubert and Ina Walberg, Borco-Marken-Import, Hamburg;

Silvia Gasperi, Pernod Ricard Deutschland, Cologne;

Gabriele Zapfe, Campari, Oberhaching;

Marlene Elvira Seitz, Caipiu one world drink, Bindlach

Picture credits

The editor and the publisher have made every effort throughout the production process to identify all owners of image rights. Persons and institutions, whom it may not have been possible to contact and who claim rights to the images used, are asked to contact the publisher retrospectively.

All images are by Armin Faber and Thomas Pothmann, with the exception of:

© akg-images: 10, 16, 34, 35, 42, 196 l.; akg-images/De Agostini Pict. Lib. 12; akg-images/Joseph Martin: 18; akg-images/Erich Lessing: 30; akg-images/Bianconero: 36; akg-images/WARNER BROTHERS/Album: 43

© Herzog August Bibliothek Wolfenbüttel: Mf 4° 5: 20

© Wilhelm-Fabry-Museum, Hilden: 21 b.

© BNIC: 22

© Arnold Holstein Destillationstechnik: 25

© Martini, Martini & Rossi Historical Archives/Bacardi GmbH: 28

© Florio – Duca di Salaparuta: 29 l.

© Byrrh/Pernod Ricard: 29 r.

© Emmanuel Picault and Ludwig Godefroy, architects, M.N.Roy, Mexico City, photographer Ramiro Chaves, chicbyaccident.com, ludwiggodefroy.com: 32, 51

© Peter F. Heering: 33

© Grand Hotel Esplanade Berlin: 37

© Raffles, www.raffles.com/singapore/: 38

© Raffles, www.raffles.com/dubai/: 39 r.

© Taj Tashi Hotel, Bhutan, www.tajhotels.com: 39 l.

© The Berkeley, www.the-berkeley.co.uk: 44/45

© DW5/Bernard Khoury, www.bernardkhoury.com: 46

© 3GATTI, Shanghai, www.3gatti.com: 47

© Christopher Cypert, The Ritz-Carlton Hotel Company, Hong Kong: 48

© Ice Bar & Hotels, London, www.belowzerolondon.com: 49 t.

© Andrew Loiterton, The Ritz-Carlton Hotel Company, Hong Kong, www.ritzcarlton.com/en/: 49 b.

© Il Bar, Bulgari Hotel & Residences London, www.bulgarihotels.com/en-us/london/: 50 t., 82

© The Cosmopolitan of Las Vegas, www.cosmopolitanlasvegas.com: 50 b.

© UBIK, Paris, www.starck.com: 52, 53

© Campari Deutschland GmbH, Oberhaching: 88 l.

© Fernet-Branca: 88 r.

© André Dominé: 94 l.

© Jack Daniel's/Brown-Forman: 98, 99

© Borco, Russian Standard Vodka: 108, 109

© Borco, Sierra Tequila: 112, 113

© Borco, De Kuyper Liqueure: 118, 119

© Borco, Heaven Hill Distilleries: 132, 133

© Miguel Torres S.A: 137

© Pernod Ricard Deutschland: 146

© Engenho Terra Vermelha, with the kind permission of Caipiu one world drink: 159 l. t., l. b.

© Pithoi Weinimporteur, Caipiu one world drink: 159 r. t.

© Agroindustria Colonia Nova, with the kind permission of Caipiu one world drink: 159 r. b.

© Michael Quack: 166, 168, 169

© Jas Hennessy & Co Collections historiques: 178, 179

© Musée de la Grande Chartreuse: 186

© Bacardi GmbH: 187

© Flensburger Schifffahrtsmuseum: 196 r.